DESTINED TO WIN

STORIES ABOUT HOW TO WIN DESPITE STRUGGLES AND DISAPPOINTMENTS!

AN ANTHOLOGY BY DR. MARY SEGARS

ISBN: 978-0-9985511-1-1

DESTINED TO WIN

Introduction

Dr. Mary Segars

*Best Seller Author/International
Speaker/Leadership & Transformational Coach*

This Destined to Win Anthology has caused me to really appreciate, even more deeply, the power of resilience. These seventeen amazing women were bold enough to tell their own experiences to win in life, despite anything that tried to hinder them.

It is an honor to lead this Destined to Win Anthology where these women bared their soul and wrote about their experiences in life. For many, that's not an easy thing to do because of hurt or shame. As you read these stories, I'm sure many can relate to what they encountered in life. As we all know that struggles, disappointments, tragedies, and setbacks are very common in everyone lives; however, the difference is how these women responded, acted, or reacted to those unforeseen or uncontrollable instances. They shared their stories with transparency and truth which allowed the readers to understand what they went through or endured, and to feel their emotions, pain or hurt. Thank God they didn't stop with just talking about the problems or the issues in their lives, they shared how those situations did not deter them from overcoming those obstacles!

One of the promises in the Bible reminds me of the resolve of these amazing women who told their truth and is leaving a legacy for many generations to come – We are Destined to Win. In 2 Corinthians 4:8 -9, 16 (NIV) states:

> *"We are hard pressed on every side, but not crushed; perplexed, but not in despair; persecuted, but not abandoned; struck down, but not destroyed. Therefore, we do not lose heart. Though outwardly we are wasting away, yet inwardly we are being renewed day by day."*

I would like to encourage every reader to know that you are more than a conqueror and you can overcome circumstances and situations, just like these contributing authors written about their own disappointments or mishaps. Know this for certain, you were **Destined to Win!**

Dr. Mary Segars
Visionary of Destined to Win
WEBSITE: www.segarsconsultgroup.com
EMAIL: marysegars737@gmail.com
FACEBOOK: www.facebook.com/mary.segars1
LINKEDIN: www.linkedin.com/in/marysegars

The Courage to Speak... Up

Rev. Ann Pollard Adams

"Please, Mr. Custard, please don't make me go!" The words to that old song were a fearful soldier's battle cry. His outcry of fear and terror was a stark reminder of the fear I faced with what was about to happen in my life.

"Please don't make me go! I don't wanna stay at their house, Momma! I don't like the way her husband looks at me!" His shifty eyes undressed me. I was only four years old when he commented on my cute little butt and cute little legs.

"One day, she's gonna grow up to be a hot little momma," he said to my parents on a regular basis during friendly visits. I dreaded hearing the unwelcome attention. "She's gonna be something else when she grows up. Yeah, boy," he said. He smacked his alcohol-smeared lips while his deceptive eyes scanned over my body.

On that dreaded night, I pleaded with my mother to allow me to go to the Detroit Tigers baseball game with the rest of the family. I did not want to be left behind to stay with relatives while everyone else went to the baseball game. "I wanna go to the Tigers game too!"

I was warned, "girls don't need to go to baseball games, 'cause baseball is for the boys only," my brother said. I reluctantly gave in and stayed the night, with the promise of a new outfit to wear on Easter Sunday.

I dreaded being left at the apartment of the shifty-eyed relative. He crept into the bedroom that night during the deafening silence. Everyone in the apartment was asleep. I only pretended to be asleep. I felt the covers being peeled away from my little four-year-old body. I felt the searing heat of his uninvited manhood that invaded the rear of my innocence.

My body was taut yet trembled in fear. The traumatizing moments of this violation had lasting effects on my well-being. Children were taught to be seen and not to be heard. Who would believe a child's allegations against an adult anyway?

This traumatic encounter occurred more than seventy years ago. It almost deterred me from reaching my destiny today. I suffered from a lack of trust with some adults, an inability to forgive others of their trespasses, and a fear of speaking up for myself well into adulthood. Many years later, a friend spoke up on my behalf, which helped me overcome the stumbling block of fear en route to my destiny.

Would you agree that we have all experienced roadblocks or barriers to our personal or professional growth? Perhaps you were challenged by a situation that appeared to delay, abort, or block your quest for upward mobility. Whatever your challenge may be, we have all experienced an event in our lives when we could have spoken up yet did not for whatever reason.

Dear readers, from the challenges I faced, please consider the importance of encouraging ourselves, our mentees, and others we encounter to speak up for the voiceless. In the words of Nelson Mandela (July 18, 1918), "I learned that courage is not the absence of fear but the triumph over it. The brave man is not he who feels afraid, but he who conquers that fear."

In the face of so much human suffering wrought by evil people, life begs the question, why are so many bad things happening to good people? John Stuart Mill (1867) reminds us... "that for evil to succeed, all it takes is for good men to do nothing."

The Good Book reminds us that we must speak up for those who cannot speak up for themselves. (Holy Bible, Proverbs 31:8-9 NIV).

We are to be intercessors and advocates for the voiceless. Esther, for example, rose from a Jewish orphanage to meet her destiny as the Queen who spoke up. She spoke up on behalf of her people at the risk of losing her own life. (Holy Bible, Esther 7:1-4.NIV)

When you look back over your life, think of an incident or occasion where you needed someone to speak up for you. Have you had to advocate for someone unable to speak for themselves? When you are destined to win, God knows the plans he has for you. Fear not, for God will send someone who has the courage to speak up on your behalf.

I am grateful to those who reached out to speak up for me. Take courage my friend; the Good Book clearly calls for Christians to "speak up for those who cannot speak for themselves... to speak up and judge fairly, defend the rights of the poor and needy..." (Prov.31:8-9 NIV)

As we speak up in support of those children or others unable to speak for themselves, we are answering a call from on high. We are destined to win the battles that are barriers to fulfilling our destiny in life. For instance, you might wonder, how can I triumph over fear? Learning to forgive was a fearful hurdle for me. The evil that I suffered as a child held me hostage from my freedom to soar. I found it difficult to forgive my perpetrator and move forward. What about you?

I had to learn that as a practicing Christian, I was obligated to forgive the evil one. After all, I believe that if we do not forgive others, God will not forgive us. Do you agree? Most of us recite the Lord's Prayer daily, "...and forgive us our trespasses, as we forgive those who trespass against us..." (Matthew 6:9-13 ESV). As an adult, while sitting in a small group session at Ecumenical Theological Seminary in Detroit, Michigan, it became clear that I had to forgive those who did trespass against me to move forward. I was able to face my fear. I feared speaking up for myself even as an adult. I could not wait to get to a quiet place to pray over how to forgive the individual who robbed me of my innocence. Boy, oh boy, was that ever a freeing experience. Scary but freeing. I was able to move forward as my ministry grew stronger.

Though difficult for me, The Lord equipped me with the non-judgmental words to speak as I made the reluctant phone call, to say, "you know, I forgive you for what you did to me when I was four-years-old."

He did not deny it. His reply was, "no, you were much older than that!"

"It's ok; I did not call to pass judgment, I called to let you know that God forgives you, and so do I. Please forgive me for my anger against you."

He finally said he was sorry about what happened. I repeated, "God has forgiven you, and I forgive you, too!" I quickly got off the phone to maintain my goodwill and composure. I thank God today for the courage to speak up for myself.

Would you agree, my fellow believers, we have, at some point in our journey, pondered the question, why do bad things happen to good people? Perhaps not only in our journey but for those with whom we minister to. When we are faced with the right thing to do, we are urged to advocate for others. Moses in the Bible, at the risk of losing his own life, is remembered as a spokesperson for the Hebrews (his people). Though he felt unworthy, he was able to confront Pharaoh with the battle cry, "Let my people go!" With God's help and several plagues later, his people escaped from their Egypt.

In seeking our destiny, we are obligated to take courage and speak up for the voiceless.

What about today's time? Yes, we are called to speak up! In recent history, 17-year-old Darnella Frazier had the courage to speak up on behalf of a dying man (George Floyd). Her courageous voice came forth as a video account and eyewitness of a truth for the whole world to witness. Our call to action today, my friends, is to take courage, speak up! When life begs the question, what will we do when we don't know what to do?

We are destined to win, despite the crisis and traumatic events in life. We are obligated to speak up for those unable to speak for themselves.

In the George Floyd case, the spokesperson's actions allowed her to remain calm. I am reminded of a poem entitled "If." This poem inspires us all in times of crisis. "If you can keep your head when all about you is losing theirs... If you can trust yourself when all men doubt you,... If you can wait and not get tired of waiting... If you can meet with triumph and disaster..."(Rudyard Kipling, Rewards and Fairies, Doubleday, Paige and Co. 1910). Darnella Frazier kept her head during a most critical time. Perhaps this poem can serve as a ministry tool.

When we are doubtful, discouraged, in crisis, and at risk of losing hope, Langston Hughes reminds us in his poem, Mother to Son (Langston Hughes, Crisis Magazine 1922), "Life for me ain't been no crystal stair...." Through the dialogue of the mother-to-son, Langston Hughes retorts that life is like a stairway, a bare one with tacks in it, but keep reaching and keep climbing until you reach the top. We must meet new challenges with courage. This poem has been an inspiration for me. Hopefully, it will help you as well.

My dear brothers and sisters, be encouraged today. Let us act upon our faith though we don't know what lies ahead. Let us move forward faithfully and be the spark that ignites the downtrodden. Take courage, my fellow believers, speak for others who are unable to speak for themselves. Trust God, speak up, especially for those who are voiceless and in need of the courage to go on. Remember, courage is not the absence of fear but the triumph over it. Be courageous. Speak up! You are destined to win!

Annie Adams is an anointed woman of God who has been in ministry for more than 30 years. She pastors at Holy Ground M.B.C, Detroit, Michigan. She believes that God's love will save you and can transform you from ordinary to extraordinary. Pastor Adams' educational pursuits have earned her a Ph.D. from Union University in Cincinnati, Ohio. She is the author of Project W.E.B. (Wee Educational Broadcasters). Adams is a Distinguished Toastmaster with Toastmasters International. Dr. Adams is a retired educator from the Detroit Board of Education. She has taught and mentored many students from preschool to adult education. She has been recognized by the Detroit Board of Education as having piloted a teen parenting prevention program. Adams has ministered as the volunteer chaplain for Veterans Administration and is a board member of ARISE! Detroit. Many can attest that Adams was blessed with the innate ability to make positive impacts on the lives of others. Her compassion is infectious. As a humble servant, she has provided spiritual care and counseling to all she encounters.

Removing The Mask So That You Can Walk Into Greatness

Kimberly M. Branche

You hear the words being told to you all the time – "you were created for this, you have the tools, it's your time, just take the leap of faith, walk into your calling, I see great things coming from you, and it's your season," and for a moment you believe them. Then reality sits along with the negative self-talk, insecurities, doubt, anxiety, and fear of the unknown. You start comparing yourself to others and asking yourself questions like, "who do you think you are?" You know you do not like talking in front of people. You don't feel equipped to get out in front of everyone. You wonder, "what will they think of me?" and contemplate taking another course until you are ready.

I am describing my experience. These are the things I have said to myself and empowering words of the people in my circle. I want to share how I dealt with the pressure of everyone's expectations and my own reality to show how I learned how to tap into everything on the inside that helped me to keep going. These strategies kept me going when I wanted to throw in the towel or hide from everyone because they believed in me while I was overthinking. Not only was the pressure from everyone getting to me, but I was also dealing with a lot of emotional baggage, including health issues, family loss, the past, a toxic work environment, and trying to be everything for everyone. So, I wore a mask, but I learned a daily practice that helped me to remove the mask and walk into my purpose. I call it the "F Factor."

Before we can talk about how I overcame, let's get to the root of the issues that started all of my insecurities, self-doubt, and the need to wear a mask. It started during my childhood. Our younger years are when we develop a foundation, confidence, self-esteem and are taught the things we need to succeed in life. I believe my parents did the best they could, but I learned some very bad habits, including carrying emotional baggage. No one taught me how to release it or how not to pick it up. I carried the baggage of my parent's divorce, my dad's suicide attempt, my family's struggles, mental and physical abuse, damaging talk about our family by my family, and grief.

I never thought about the future because I did not think I'd live to see it. I remember just going through the motions after being kicked out of the house my senior year of high school. Fortunately, my brother and his wife took me in. While most of my classmates were looking forward to graduating and the future, I found out my dad had lung cancer. I never prayed so hard in my life for God to spare him. He died on February 7, and I wanted to die with him. I couldn't deal with everything anymore, and I felt alone.

I will never forget the day Lil Mike, who was also living with my brother and his wife at the time, walked into my room and saw me with a gun. The next thing I knew, my brother had grabbed the gun from me. I guess it was a cry for help, but I did not get help. If anything, it made things worse. I put my mask on and kept going.

A few months later, my maternal grandmother suddenly passed away from a massive stroke. She was always there for me, especially in the hard times. Less than two years later, my paternal grandmother passed away from a brain tumor. It seemed like everyone was leaving. I decided to do the same, another one of my traits, running. I should have been a track star from all the times I ran from my reality instead of facing them. After high school, I joined the Army, got married, and vowed never to look back and to leave my baggage in Louisiana, I thought.

After being stationed in Japan for ten years, we returned to the United States and moved to Arizona. Our family had expanded from just my husband and me to an additional three kids. We were back in the US and excited to be setting up roots. We found a church home where my husband and I were heavily involved in ministry. I taught Youth bible study and Praise Dancing while he was a Deacon, and we taught Sunday School together. Our kids were also involved in community programs, and life was good. What I did not realize we were burning ourselves out. As a parent, I wanted to be involved, so I volunteered for everything. My husband and I were both pursuing our master's degrees, and he was transitioning out of the military.

During that time, all hell was breaking loose in my body. I began losing my hair, so I went natural before it was a thing. I was sensitive to the sun and had become extremely fatigued. I scheduled an appointment with the doctor, and after several tests I was diagnosed with Lupus. I remember thinking, "oh no, not me. I have things to do, and Lupus is not one of them." By the time I left the doctor's office, he had given me seven different medications to reduce the inflammation and slow down the progression of the disease.

I remember the doctor telling me to quit working. I felt like I had the weight of the world on my shoulders, and everything was collapsing. Typical me, I went into overdrive using my volunteer work as a distraction, a mask. My mother also became ill, suffering from a stroke, and I became her power attorney trying to make decisions for her from another state. Kim to the rescue, they say, she's the fixer. Watching the woman I admired and looked up to suffer was heartbreaking. Deep down, I wondered if I was following in her footsteps with the baggage or was I looking at my future self.

Things began to calm down. My autoimmune system was getting better, and the mask I had been wearing was still holding things together for me. Life was good. Then I hit a point where I could not hold it together anymore. I was tired again, and things were slipping at work. The environment was toxic, which did not help my situation. I had taught my body to tolerate the pain by pushing forward without emotions. I went back to the doctor, but this time was worse. I was diagnosed with Sjogren's, Fibromyalgia, and Multiple Myeloma. My doctor said she could treat me for everything except Multiple Myeloma. I was referred to a Hematology/Oncology Specialists.

After more labs, pet scans, and biopsies, it was official; I had Multiple Myeloma, cancer of the plasma cells. My Oncologist wanted to start an aggressive plan of six months of chemotherapy and then a stem cell transplant since my cancer was in the early stages. I went through the process of getting my appointments scheduled for the next six months, prescriptions were sent to the pharmacy, and I was mentally preparing for my chemotherapy and life with cancer. Then my insurance company denied my treatment three times. They even denied a Clinical trial offered by the top Multiple Myeloma Specialist at the Mayo Clinic. This went on for about six months, and I remember my husband telling me to tap into my faith. He reminded me that I needed to start practicing what we had been preaching. However, I just wanted the cancer gone from my body.

My husband asked me if I ever thought God was working it out on my behalf, and that was why the doors were closing. Years ago, we had learned a valuable lesson about being patient and waiting on God. Being patient required me to trust the process but also to get centered and change my mindset. Making decisions based on emotions, fear, and impulses was not effective. I had to believe that God was my provider and keeper. When my mindset changed about not having chemotherapy to remove the cancer, I realized it was a GOD thing. I knew I was going to be okay even though I still had cancer in my body. I remember the doctors saying they did not understand. At that moment, I realized I was given a second chance at life, and I needed to figure out what I was going to do with it. I had gone through so much, and I was tired of wearing the mask.

Even when I was going through all the medical issues, I still had family and friends encouraging me to keep going but to slow down. For me slowing down was not an option. I had dreams I wanted to fulfill because I knew God was calling me to greater things by giving me a second chance. I didn't believe he had brought me this far to leave me, and that became my motto. I was going to turn my mess into a message, and that required me to step out on faith and face my fears by walking in my purpose.

To conquer one of my fears, public speaking, I took a leap and auditioned to be part of an organization called A 2nd Act that helps cancer survivor share their journey before a live audience. Sharing my journey not only helped me heal but it was also helping other cancer warriors heal. I never imagined being on the news or doing speaking engagements, but I learned to overcome that fear. I had to step out on FAITH! Now I have learned to use my voice to educate others on wellness and self-care. My mask started coming off as I began to walk into my 2nd Acts with faith and knowing what I was called to do, empower others.

This is the "F Factor" that helped me remove my MASK:

1.   **Fear**. It destroys dreams and realities CONQUER IT with positive thinking over the negative thoughts.

2.   **Forgiveness**. I learn to forgive the little girl in me that was hurting from all the pain, loss and thinking she wasn't good enough. I learned to forgive all the people that hurt me intentionally and unintentionally. I was holding on to baggage and it was mentally and physically hurting me.

3.   **Forget**. After I forgave myself and the people that hurt me, I had to leave it in the past.

4.   **Faith**. I had to learn to speak faith-filled words over my life as it is a DAILY journey. Life and death are in

the power of your tongue. Speak these words daily until you believe them:

- I am an overcomer
- I am a victor over my illness
- I belong here
- I am who God says that I am

5. **Family**. My family is what motivated, inspired, and kept me when I needed them the most. My husband poured into me with the Word when I had self-doubt. Surround yourself with family members you can be honest and transparent about what you are going through so that healing can begin.

6. **Friends**. Your circle should be individuals that encourage, inspire, and are honest with you. Remember, iron sharpens iron.

When you are hit with so many things, you tend to wonder why these things are happening. Get real and be honest with yourself so that you can move forward. Learn to accept what has taken place, let go of baggage that requires you to wear the mask, seek therapy to deal with past hurts, change your mindset, and speak faith-filled words over your life. Remember, some trials come to make us stronger. Without cancer, who knows what my life would have been like, but it allowed me to activate my FAITH and step into what I know I was DESTINED to do, and that's WIN. But I had to first remove the mask to walk into my GREATNESS.

Kimberly M. Branche is a Personal Development and Leadership Coach, Certified John Maxwell Coach, Trainer, and Speaker; and CEO of Branche Basu Boutique. She launched Branche Basu Boutique, a Natural Bath and Body care line to promote wellness and self-care after her cancer diagnosis. As a Multiple Myeloma survivor, she advocates by hosting bone marrow drives, speaking engagements, and awareness events. Kimberly is a contributing author in Survivors Take A Real Stage Vol 2., which inspired her to start writing her first book, Breaking Silence.

As a coach she founded Beyond The Salute to offer personal and leadership development coaching and training to military members, spouses, and civilians. Kimberly combined years of expertise and life experiences, as a federal employee, military veteran, military spouse, and passion into helping other navigate life. She holds a Bachelor of Science in Social Psychology and Master of Arts in Marriage and Family Counseling; Kimberly can be counted on to guide members toward growth and living life BEYOND THE SALUTE. For more information about Kimberly go to www.kimberlybranche.com.

A Legacy of Love

Tonya L. Carter

I WASN'T SUPPOSED TO BE HERE!

"… Grandaddy, can I keep my baby?"

This is the tail end of the story, but I was shocked to hear it when I was almost 10. Don't get me wrong; I'd done the math when I was about 8 when I realized that my mom looked waaaay younger than everyone else's mom. She'd had me when she was sixteen!

However, love is a powerful emotion. You know how songs say it can move mountains, reach the moon and stars, or that there are ribbons in the sky for our love? That is the kind of love that my parents had when they started on an early journey of parenthood before they were grown-ups. However, the love of God, family, and faith in the Word made this a journey they did not regret.

Because of that love of God, I must talk about love as described in the Bible and the Greek terms for how I learned them. These types of love not only helped them to survive but thrive and pass down a legacy of love to their children, grandchildren, and great-grandchildren.

First, there is Eros (AIR-ohs) love (Proverbs 5:18-19; 1 Corinthians 7:5). This is the passionate love that brought my parents together. They became an item when my dad was dating my aunt. SMH! But love could not be stopped, albeit too soon.

Then there's Storge (STOR-jay) love (Romans 12:10). My Mom describes how the family had love "bouncing off the walls." They were poor but had no idea. Despite that, the family had laughs, hugs, and kisses to go around and then some, and supported each other through thick and thin.

Next is Philia (FILL-ee-uh) love (John 13:35). This brotherly love is the kind that unites believers. Do you remember the days when you spent ALL DAY in church on Sundays? The fellowship started with breakfast at church, then Sunday School, then services, then dinner where everyone brought a dish, then home to get ready for school or work the next day. We were a community. A village. And this village helped to raise a child.

Finally, the best love of all is Agape (Uh-GAH-pay) love (John 3:16). God's love is unconditional. This is the model for unselfish love, living with your arms, hands, and heart open. Love that makes you sacrifice for others. Just like my parents did.

While growing up, I saw first-hand how every one of these types of love impacted our family. This offered a solid platform to create an opportunity for a young couple to more than survive with a surprise on the way.

I WASN'T SUPPOSED TO BE HERE.

I'd heard the story several times because my mother was transparent, truthful, and unapologetic about her choices. Namely, keeping me when some others didn't want her to. Here's the rest of the story:

My mom's aunt and uncle lived in DC. Our very large extended family lived in the DMV area and were very close. However, some were very concerned with propriety. Her aunt & uncle decided it would be in her best interest to "take care of" me while my mom was there to visit. Mom described to me her last days visiting with them over the summer.

While visiting my aunt and uncle over the summer during a weekday ministry that helped to take food out to the community, we headed to visit those who were going to help cook the meals. I was wearing an oversized striped shirt to hide my pooch, but they noticed and started to whisper to each other. My aunt and uncle were so embarrassed and planned to help "take care of" the issue. I told them that I was looking forward to the weekend to visit my grandmother & grandfather since my mom was away helping another family member or friend. Little did my aunt and uncle know that I didn't plan to return. When I returned home, I asked my grandaddy if I could have you, and he said, "Of course you can keep your baby!"

This story became a catalyst to who I've become.

In my first authoring endeavor, Take Your Turn!: A Leadership Guide to Success for Young Women, I wrote about having a "super why" in Chapter 5, titled Needs & Wants. I created this term to capture the important reasons that helped motivate me to maintain my priorities and stay on track when distractions tried to block my progress.

If I wanted a successful future, I thought that delayed gratification might be something I needed to practice regularly. It meant choosing to complete assignments before going to hang out with friends. It also meant not getting too serious about a boyfriend until I'd accomplished some of my most important goals. That's the "super why." It's that ultimate reason that drives you to achieve something. For me, it was getting into the college of my choice with a scholarship so that my parents wouldn't need to help me pay for it. I was prioritizing and focusing! These strategies would help me to stay on track to achieve the dream.

I had a singular focus with my "super why" in place. I would be the first woman in my family to graduate from a four-year college. However, I didn't want just any college, I wanted to go to a highly accredited college on a scholarship so that my parents wouldn't need to sacrifice financially for me to gain a quality education, or I wouldn't have a large student loan to pay while starting my career. For me, it wasn't a matter of if but when and how I'd accomplish this. That singular-minded focus served me well.

I WASN'T SUPPOSED TO BE HERE?

As I wrote on this topic of "super why" in my book, I asked myself why I was so hyper-focused throughout high school. Yes, the "super why" helped me avoid distraction and disruptions, but why was this so important. What was the source of it all? I even had a mantra in high school of putting the "functional before the fun." Years later, I asked my parents why this was so important to them, and they both laughed and said I'd done it to myself. Dad commented, "Think about it. Your sisters and brother didn't take the same path. Why would we have a different set of rules for each of you?"

OMG! I really did do this to myself! So, again I ask, "Why?" It wasn't a bad choice. It was the right one for me, but I really wanted to understand why I was so laser-focused on my goal.

Then, one day my Mom called me and said she was crying (happy) tears after she and Dad listened to an interview of me about my book, and she was "so proud to be my mother." Cue the screeching tires from braking with both feet! It hit me full force why I was so laser-focused as a teen and even tend to plan everything in my life now!

I'M SUPPOSED TO BE HERE!

I realized that the main reason that my "super why" was so clear for me is because I never wanted my mom and dad to regret the decision to keep me! While my mom was concerned that we were embarrassed to have such young parents, we appreciated parents who were able to relate, physically participate in sports with us, not to mention the sacrifices they made to put food on the table and a nice roof over our heads. They exposed us to sports and other activities to keep us too busy for distractions. Dad was the primary provider, but mom helped financially as well as maintained the household and make sure that we were immersed in the church and the Word.

My path developed as an extension to their journey. I asked mom's thoughts on this, and she replied:

"We fall down, but we get back up. It's not what you can't do, but what you will do. God doesn't make mistakes. He allows things to happen. Children are gifts from Him! He has always protected me, especially when He gifted me with my children."

This young woman had faith in God's plan and His purpose for her, her children, and her relationship with my dad from the very beginning. More than whispering relatives. More than the nay-sayers. The love of God, the love and support from her immediate family, and the love for her unborn child gave her the strength to push past fears and doubts. That is not an easy feat. Not everyone would make the same decision if faced with the same situation. But I, for one, am glad she did.

Ultimately, I am supposed to be here because He created a legacy of love in our family. And when God has a purpose for you, and you fulfill it, no matter the initial circumstances, you are DESTINED TO WIN in the end (Jeremiah 29:11; 32:19; Proverbs 16:4)!

Tonya L. Carter is an author, Veteran, Human Resource Management Executive, Business Owner, Leadership Consultant, and Change Agent. Her primary passion is using her talents to help others reach their potential. She was raised with a family legacy of serving others, so this direction was a natural fit. Her book "Take Your Turn!" became a #1 National Bestseller. Although she is an HR Professional, she started as an Engineer. After West Point, she served as an Army Engineer Officer for 11 years. However, her ability to lead others effectively was recognized as a transferrable skill to HR while working for General Motors. Exposure to this new way to help others sparked the desire to return to school for her Master of Training & Development with a focus on Organizational Development at Oakland University. She enjoys serving the community with her church and sorority, reading, and playing golf for fun.

Note: If you liked this and want to read more by this author, check out Take Your Turn!: A Leadership Guide to Success for Young Women. Along with this Destined to Win anthology, it can be ordered at www.apearlplusconsulting.com.

Determined To Be Great

Denise Cochran, #1 Best-Selling Author

des·tined - (of a person's future) developing as though according to a plan. Preordained.

When there is a purpose for your life, something you are destined to have or become, nothing can hinder you. My determination started in me at conception. Let's talk about fertilization. The process goes like this:

A pregnancy starts with fertilization when a woman's egg joins with a man's sperm. Fertilization usually takes place in a fallopian tube that links an ovary to the uterus. If the fertilized egg successfully travels down the fallopian tube and implants in the uterus, an embryo starts growing.

I'm sure you are wondering why I'm sharing this with you. I want to plant this seed to understand why I am Destined To Win and Determined To Be Great. My determination started from the point of conception. I will give a short version of this story. My mom has six children, five boys and one girl, her baby. My mom always wanted a girl, although she kept being blessed with boys. Her pregnancy with my youngest brother was difficult; and the delivery was even harder. It was so difficult; she was sick for a year after she had him. During that time, my mom decided to have a tubal ligation (tied her fallopian tubes) so that she would not have more children, especially after the trauma from the last baby. Well, about nine years later, a dream from her past came true. On August 1st, she gave birth to her baby girl. Yes, her tubes became untied, and here I am. To me, this was a birth of purpose. I made it through what medically was not supposed to happen. So even at conception, against all odds, I was determined to be here. In life, we all face things that can make us or break us. I've had a near-death experience. I had lost so much blood; my blood count was three and falling. The doctors said I should have had a heart attack and couldn't believe I had driven myself to the hospital in my condition. But I was determined to get help. I had to be given nine units of blood through a transfusion, and I had to have emergency surgery. The doctors weren't sure if I would make it to or even through the surgery at the rate I was losing blood. But I survived; I was determined to be here.

de·ter·mined - *having made a firm decision and being resolved not to change it.*

Let me ask you, have you ever been in the wrong place at the wrong time? Better yet, have you ever been somewhere you had ABSOLUTELY no business being?

I have. Picture this. I was waiting to hear about these $100 bills. I tried to put them in the slot machine, but it wouldn't take it. I tried to put it in the change machine, and it wouldn't take it either. So, I took it to the woman behind the cage. I asked if she could tell me if there was something wrong with those bills. She was taking a long time, so I asked was everything okay, but NO RESPONSE. I could hear the slot machines ringing in the background (ding-ding-ding) and people screaming "YES," from winning on the machines. I could even hear a dealer yell out, "STRAIGHT FLUSH WE HAVE A WINNER!"

Then, I noticed two security guards standing on the side of me, they weren't close, but I could see them in my peripheral vision. I asked the woman again, "is something wrong?" FINALLY, she looked at me as if I were a criminal and replied, "yes, this money is COUNTERFEIT." I felt like my heart had dropped to my shoes. By then, six security guards were surrounding me, and Joe, the head of security who knew me, and told me they would have to handcuff me. I felt like someone had just punched me in my stomach. I am a recovering gambling addict and that was me several years ago inside of a casino. I had just received those bills from a department store as a refund. I was experiencing what's considered a relapse in my addiction, and I had gone straight to the casino with those crisp $100 bills. After an investigation by the State Police, I was cleared of any responsibility. But what a lesson. I had no business being inside that casino after asking God to free me from the addiction and promising Him all that I would do if He did.

When we hear the word addiction – the most common things we think about are drugs and alcohol. But addiction is the condition of being addicted to a particular substance, thing, or activity. So yes, it could be gambling, food, sex, shopping, or even social media. It can be anything we allow ourselves to become enslaved to.

Gambling had such a stronghold on my life that it began to feel normal like I wasn't doing anything wrong or that it was causing harm. I started going to the casino as an escape. It was the one place I could go to get away because I was being pulled in so many different directions. The casino allowed me to be there with no worries or concerns. There were no deadlines to meet, no answering questions, no expectations, only me putting money on the table. It was the place I felt the most relaxed. It started as a place of pure enjoyment, a pleasure trip, but then it turned into something detrimental, the place I allowed to destroy my life.

Be careful with your destiny and determination because when it's innate, the same energy can be used on things that are not positive and prosperous. Being such a determined person also played a part in my quest to always be a winner when gambling. Don't get me wrong, the gambling behavior and the addictive mentality were key factors and very real but having such determination, many times I felt like I was not going to be defeated by those gambling losses and would keep trying and trying and to no good end. I have experienced losing it all several times living with my gambling addiction. I wasn't sure if I could bounce back from the financial ruin I created for myself, but I knew there was a reason I was still standing.

In my past career, I was a Financial Analyst. I sat right next to the Chief Financial Officer and the Controller. I was in control of managing and budgeting the client's money, but I struggled with managing my own money. My bosses had no idea I gambled. I suffered from the addiction for 14 years and didn't realize I had a problem. I didn't just gamble and constantly lose. I also hit REALLY BIG on the poker table a number of times. But, I've been on the other side more often than I had cared to

34

admit. I've had days where I went into the casino, put $5k-$10k on the table and lost it all, and then found myself in VIP picking up my BMW scrounging around for $2 to put gas in my tank. I've been in the casino with thousands on the table, winning big. Then the losing streak hits, and before you know it, I've been in the casino for two days. It was mind-boggling trying to understand how something that seems so enjoyable could turn into something so detrimental. Gambling was the hurricane in my life.

Having great talent and being the Jack of all trades was something I used to take pride in. Over the years, I learned that having my hands in so many things and seeing things through to the finish line was a problem for me. Having compulsive and impulsive behavior kept me in a bit of a fog at times. I would feel glad and so accomplished that I was able to master (in my mind) so many things, not realizing I was creating what could be considered a black hole, where things just hover around me, incomplete, and then disappear into this blank space unaccounted for.

When you decide to change your life, it is a battle that is not fought just once; it is ongoing and very intense. Transition can be a deep, revealing, and lonely place. It can also be a place of release, forgiveness, and happiness. When the heart and soul know this is what has to take place to improve your life, to live the life God destined for you, there is no other way. You've tried other ways, remember? They didn't work. This transformation does not necessarily come with simple instructions or infallible attempts. Every level of transition is different for each individual; instructions for change are tailored to fit you. The keys to this transition, this awakening of the spirit, this renewing of the mind, this uncomfortable swing in life, is commitment and trust.

Commitment to enter this unleashing and the trust that God will see you through it victoriously. The commitment to allow the change to reconstruct the patterns for your life and the trust that God has His hands on you during the reconstruction. The commitment to allowing the discomfort of shedding the old you, the old thoughts, the old actions, the old way of life, and the trust that God will not let your discomfort be your dwelling place but a healing place. The commitment to resist temptation in any form allowing the feeling of truth and righteousness to shine forth and the trust that God knows your heart and will support you in your efforts to live in His image. The commitment to isolate yourself to allow purification and positioning and the trust that God will have your new structured life waiting for you when you emerge from your solitude. The commitment to move on from past relationships and experiences and the trust that God will reveal the team that He hand-picked for you. The commitment to allowing the belief in who you are and how strong you are and the trust that God will remove all self-doubt and fear.

You see, when you commit to doing something that you have set your mind to, it is your conscientious decision that nothing will stop you from reaching the end result. You are determined. When you trust in God, it is your commitment to believing that He loves you and He will never fail.

Determined to be great are words to live by. The road traveled may have been hard, and you may have even been knocked down, but it didn't knock you out. Dust wipes off regret does not. Get up, dust yourself off and use your determination to try again. You are destined to win!

Committing to a path of change may be lonely and uncomfortable, but by following the correct instruction and through prayer and persistence, there will be a sense of completeness, a sense of fullness, a sense of wholeness, a sense of comfort beyond the imagination. There will be a renewing of things that have been deadened. There will be an unleashing of strength, power, and passion as you pursue your purpose in life. There will be a new spirit that resonates on the inside and will become reflective on the outside, through words and actions.

Today, I have moved past the things that hindered me from moving in the things destined for my life. I no longer gamble. I no longer work tirelessly on someone else's dream. I no longer avoid facing my fears. I have fulfilled a lifelong dream of becoming a Realtor. I am a #1 Best-Selling Author. I am a Life-Coach and a Motivational Speaker. I share this with you to encourage you, inspire you, and motivate you. When you are determined to be great, you can do anything you put your mind to. Whatever it is, do it! You truly are destined to win!

Meet Denise Cochran, #1 Best-Selling Author, Speaker, and successful REALTOR®. Denise has been successful in various positions throughout her professional career, such as Financial Analyst, Business Analyst and Procurement Engineer.

Fully supporting 2 children as a single mother and filtering through life's challenges, while feeling unfulfilled, Denise decided it was time to live in her purpose. Her near death experience which lead to emergency surgery, is how Denise came to understand, that the things we experience in life are not only for teaching us, but to serve as learning tools to inspire the lives of other people.

Denise has embarked upon new life, a new journey, and a new direction. She moved on a path of change, for improvement, for prosperity and for success. She is ready to share her story about living in her destiny. Her mantra is, Change Your Mind. Change your life. Denise is Destined to Win!

Destiny is Calling!!

Dr. Anita Davis-DeFoe

Silence filled the room as I painfully watched my mother take her final breaths. During the seventy-four years that my mother lived, she always gave untiringly to our family, the students she taught as an elementary school teacher for some 38 years, her community, her church, her sorority, and to others she met along life's pathway. I felt blessed to have been so fortunate, for my mother was always my greatest supporter, an endless fountain of encouragement.

As the reality of my loss enveloped me on that cool January night, it was a Saturday, the 8th, the year 2005 was still brand new. Up until that point, 2005 had seemed filled with endless possibilities. That entire year became a blur from that moment on.

Three hundred and sixty-eight days later, on January 3rd, 2007, the telephone rang. My sister was weeping as she said, "Anita, Daddy just died." I remember this moment as though it was yesterday. Slumping over at my desk at work and crying hysterically, on that day, I shed tears as I reflected again on the loss of my mother; now my father, a man who had been a school principal for forty-three years, a leader who had been the first African-American City Councilman in the city where I grew up, an Omega man who tried to help everyone, a man who gave me his all, and now he was gone. Here, once again, in the month of

January, I was filled with despair, and I sobbed uncontrollably at the thought of my life.

You see, to the world, it looked as though my life was full of joy, a magic carpet ride. I was married to a handsome man, but not happily. I was a Vice-President at an organization earning good money, I had a newspaper column, wrote for a magazine in the Caribbean, had a radio show, and at the time, I had written two books. But even still, in my heart, I knew that something was missing. I heard whispers each and every day. Actually, for over four years, a message, even though I tried to block it out, but it was crystal clear, always the same, "destiny is calling."

We all harbor our dreams deep with our souls. Sometimes we reflect on our dreams, and for a few minutes, we allow ourselves to think about how things could be. On other occasions, we keep them tucked away so that our dreams cannot intrude on what we are doing; after all, we are too busy living life to be inconvenienced by our dreams. When that is the case, clearly, we have not yet learned that until we follow the urging of hearts, we will be filled with discontent and longing. Finding the courage to live your dreams, while frightening, can actually turn out to be liberating. When you discover the lifework that you want to pursue, the business you want to start or embrace whatever your dream might be, your life will become so much more fulfilling that you will ask yourself, "Why did I wait so long to pursue something that truly interested me?" Too often, we allow fear, the comments of others, or our own negative self-talk to keep us from stepping out and trying to achieve what our spirits are urging us to do. Are you trying to chase your dreams away?

Throughout those years, as I struggled to chase my dreams away, the spirit said, "there is other work for you to do, you must journey far out of your comfort zone, for it is there you will discover purpose, and it is there you will truly manifest destiny. Do not be mistaken, the journey you have traveled in your yesterdays has been the preparation for your todays, and the promise of your todays and the possibilities of your tomorrows. Choose to answer the call of destiny and let your steps be ordered so that you can discover your divine pathway." On that day, in the midst of my tears of sorrow, a most precious wellspring of spiritual wisdom came forth, and the message was "do not wait for loss to come before you choose to start living."

In the following months, as I fought to get up from the pity party table and make my way in the world coping with the loss of my parents, I allowed fear to keep me tucked in my comfort zone. Questions like, what if you leave the job, what will happen to you? Will you stay in an unhappy marriage for appearance's sake or seek inner peace and joy? Will you pursue your innermost dreams, or will you choose to maintain the status quo? Are you afraid that if you pursue your dreams, you can never find another job if you need to put your entrepreneurial aspirations to the side? What would you attempt to do if you knew you would not fail?

As I pondered these questions, I continued to do as I had done for many years, and that was straddle the fence. By day and most weeks, I played my role as the organizational vice-president. By night and on weekends, I showed up at book signings, wrote for media houses, and covered all kinds of political, social, and musical events. I spoke at conferences, conducted trainings, shared at special events, and was a part-time global radio personality. Still refusing to acknowledge any of the messages I was receiving from destiny, I tried to learn how to just settle. Then it happened, something so compelling, an act that was blatantly wrong, and I knew that it was time. I would have to choose, either play the game that was being required, or create my own game and be my authentic self.

On December 17, 2007, I finally answered destiny's call, resigned from my job, and decided to give my life, destiny living a chance.

On that December day, I decided to give my heartfelt dreams a try. I decided to bet on me, and I decided to kick fear to the curb and pursue my dreams. Each of us will find ourselves confronted with pivotal decision points throughout our lives: fear or fly, test or testimony, quest, or quake, pursue or put-off, determine or defer, choose or chance, obstacle or opportunity, problem or possibility.

Have you stopped to think about the power and impact of a decision? Do you realize that the decisions you make today can impact future outcomes and generations of tomorrow? Do you clearly understand that your decisions can either give flight to your dreams or render them virtually impossible to achieve? Have you come to grips with the fact that your decisions can open or block the pathway to your ultimate destiny? The steps I took on that sunny Florida day in December profoundly changed my life and have afforded me with opportunities to work and travel, meet people across the United States and from around the world, serve and contribute to projects and programs that impact the lives of people of all ages and ethnicities. On most days, the opportunities that are bestowed upon me are a pleasant surprise, and I constantly reflect on what I would be missing if I had continued to ignore destiny's repeated calls. I think of the personal loss I would have experienced if destiny had decided to stop calling.

While in simple terms, a decision is making a choice on a particular issue, it is the human act of deriving a conclusion or making up one's mind about something; decisions are so much more. They uplift and lead us to personal greatness, or they serve to stymie and derail our progress.

Although it should come as no surprise, so much of what we achieve, so many of life's pleasures that we derive, so many things that find a resting place in our lives first begin with our decisions. Life can be viewed as a series of decisions, and we have to ask ourselves. "am I making decisions that foster my personal success, joy, and contentment?"

Our decisions should always be a course of action that accomplishes or moves us closer to our ultimate goal or serves to bring us greater inner peace. Although the decision to make is not always clear, not always painless to identify, not always easy to make, we must make a decision. Straddling the fence makes one weary. Your divine destiny is calling you, but each of us must make a choice whether we will answer. We must decide if we are going to live by choice or by chance.

When making decisions, especially as it relates to our destinies, each of us must strive not to allow irrational ideas, false assumptions, fears, unmet needs, or other fluctuating emotions to block our good decision-making abilities. Ensure that you are in touch with your honest feelings about your life, your future, and do not let self-doubt sway you from making a life-affirming decision.

While each of us is different, and we all have different decision-making styles, as humankind, we all share one commonality: every individual is a reflection of all the decisions made in their lives to date. This is rather humbling when one stops and realizes that where they are is where they choose to be.

Decisions about the use of your time, the behaviors you claim as habits, the people you call friends, the vocation that becomes your career, and the person you choose to share your life with are all pivotal decisions that we must make. These decisions either serve to enhance our lives or shatter it to shreds.

Get in the habit of systematically checking your decisions before making choices; think of this as serious business, as though your life were at stake because it is. Remember, choice is merely *C*hoosing *H*eartfelt *O*pportunities *I*ntelligently *C*onsciously *E*veryday.

Remember that destiny decisions unlock the doorway to boundless possibilities. Understand that personal success as you define it is yours. It is waiting for your arrival, and this requires us to believe in ourselves, acknowledge our dreams, and know that the resources needed to achieve the dream will arrive when needed when we seek and serve guided by purpose.

Think about it, if you get into your car without a destination in mind, where will you end up... almost anyplace. If you go into the grocery stores without a list, what will you buy... almost anything and definitely more than you intended. Both of these examples point to valuable food for thought, without direction and focus, we flounder. Thus, to achieve personal success and to win on your own terms, you must be purposeful.

What is purpose? Purpose is intent, goals, a target, or a personal aim. Purpose is identifying exactly what you seek to achieve and then developing a plan to make it happen, a plan that includes persistence, persistence, and more persistence.

The importance of purpose cannot be stressed enough. Purpose will help you focus your time and energy, purpose will help you to develop expertise in your areas of interest, purpose will help you persist in the face of obstacles, purpose will help you remain determined when people try to discourage you, and purpose will help you to achieve the inner peace that our spirits constantly seek.

At birth, divinely, we are given at least one talent, often more. The difficult part of life's journey is discovering what that talent might be and deciding to use that talent in a purposeful manner that brings us personal joy.

Our ideas and dreams are messages sent to us by our spirits to help guide the personal seeds that we sow. Most times, we let fear of failure, self-doubt, and past experiences keep us from answering these wake-up calls, wake-up calls that are indeed spiritual awakenings beckoning us to step through the gateways which lead to our unique personal opportunities.

Refuse to go through life sleepwalking and instead choose to live your life filled with purpose. Commit to finding purpose for your life, and you will become unstoppable!!!

Destiny is calling, and from my experience, I suggest that you answer the call quickly! You will be glad you did.

Remember, you only get one life, so why not choose to spend it happily doing the things that you enjoy. Be courageous and persist until you achieve your life goals and your personal dreams. Follow your heart and listen to your soul, for the treasures placed there were designed to lead you to your destiny. You truly owe it to yourself to use the talents divinely bestowed upon you in a positive fashion doing things that bring you immense joy. When you think about it, don't you really want to become the person you were destined to become? This is my daily quest, and I do it in honor of my parent's legacy in gratitude for my life, and I am certainly enjoying the journey. I wish the same for you, for destiny is your friend.

Quoted as a career development expert in Essence Magazine; a business thought solutionist in Black Enterprise Magazine; and in other publications, Dr. DeFoe is the CEO of Upshift Global, a consultancy organization and knowledge incubator that serves individuals, businesses, and non-profits. She serves as President. the India-US Virgin Islands Women's Indian Chamber of Commerce and Industry and on the Board of Advisors for Businessita, an accelerator program based in Cairo, Egypt. A John C. Maxwell Team Executive Director, Dr. DeFoe is the author of four books. In 2012, in honor of her global human development and social entrepreneurship work, she was named the first Woman Chief by the ITAM CLAN in Abwu Ibom State Nigeria. Additionally, she received the African Leadership Award from Voice Magazine in Amsterdam in 2014, and a 2015 Social Entrepreneur Leadership Award from Naijaeutv Spain for designing global social enterprises. In 2019, she received a Global Philanthropist Award from Panache Global Entertainment (PGE) London. In 2020, Dr DeFoe received a Women in Leadership Service Award at the Women's Economic Forum Cairo Egypt.

Don't Take A Backseat On Purpose

Shawntay Dixon

Can you remember riding in the back seat as a child? I have vivid childhood memories of scenic drives with my family growing up. Every Sunday, Dad and Mom packed up the family, and we headed to the east side to visit family. It seemed like quite a distance heading to our destination. I loved riding in the backseat, looking out the window, and enjoying the scenery. There were times, Dad would take us near Belle Isle, the Renaissance Center, and the Spirit of Detroit to enjoy these beautiful Detroit landmarks. These were just a few of the joys I experienced taking a backseat.

The driver is in ultimate control and carries tremendous responsibility. As the driver, you must look out not just for yourself but your passengers and others on the road. Usually, in the driver's seat, you miss the scenery and small details a back seat rider enjoys. Navigating, you don't see much beauty as you drive to your destination safely. I remember my brother and I would yell out, "did you see that?" Dad would usually respond, "see what?" There wasn't much freedom in the passenger seat either. In the passenger seat, you assisted the driver either navigating or assisting with some other assigned chore, at times not joyous. Riding in the backseat meant freedom.

Once, on our annual family trip to Georgia to visit Mom's family, I rethought taking a back seat. I especially enjoyed the drive until this particular trip. I experienced the beauty of the terrain, God's masterpieces, the lush green trees, the wildflowers that looked as though someone spray-painted a mural, and the vast hills, waterways, and mountains. We saw animals at peace going about their business. What beauty we experienced in the back seat! I'll never forget this trip. It was unusually hot all week; hotter than July was an understatement. Dad loved driving at night, "because traffic was lighter, not as many trucks as during the day." I think it was because of our vehicle's lack of air conditioning. Traveling at night made for a cooler, more joyous trip with a car full of kids who, when awake asked, "are we there yet?" a gazillion times. At least at night, the darkness and white lines that chased us on the road lulled the most hyper kid to sleep.

Again, this trip was memorable, one I will never forget. We were on our journey and rolling along fine; then, as we got somewhere between Kentucky and Tennessee, the air became particularly foggy. The more southward we traveled, the heavier the fog, like someone brought a cottony pillow to snuff us out. This fog was so great, none of us could see what was next to or in front of us. Mom beckoned Dad to slow down, to pull off the road, but he was determined to eventually drive through it.

Suddenly, white lights headed in our direction! We were in oncoming traffic! This happened so fast I could feel my heart outside my chest. I could taste danger. Time was at a standstill. There was an eerie feeling in this sea of white. Narrowly escaping tragedy, a kind truck driver appeared and navigated us to the right side. Shaking, Dad jumped off the first exit. He didn't need Mom to say anything else. Thankfully, my siblings slept soundly through the entire episode. Awake, I no longer felt joy as a backseat rider. We stayed parked until the sun rose. With the rising sun, we saw an entire parking lot full of cars and trucks that paused their journey due to the danger.

Thirty-five years later, I allowed a danger to push my life's purpose into the back seat. Just like Dad, driving stubbornly through the fog to his destination, I found myself engulfed in a fog, wondering how did I get here and how do I get out? And just like Dad, I've learned that some of life's greatest lessons come from our failures.

Taking a back seat has its appropriate place, but not when it comes to your purpose. Several years ago, I discovered my purpose. I was well on my way to walking in it. Someone I revered and held in high esteem presented an offer. He needed me to provide consulting for his business and develop a strategic plan for this 30-year-old company. Before long, I found myself moving out of a consulting role into actively participating in the execution of the plan. In hindsight, my first misstep. I really didn't have a desire to be this deeply involved, but somewhere deep down, between my gift of helping others and not wanting to disappoint, I took residence. Many said that this opportunity was a tremendous blessing, I went along. Just know when you discover your purpose; distractions are sure to follow. I was convinced that I could do what I felt in my heart I should be doing while helping this person to turn around his company. Before long, I was giving more and more of my time where I did not have the energy to pursue my purpose. He then offered the opportunity to become a minority shareholder with the promise it would be mine. I contributed sweat equity… time, talent, and commitment, to build the company. I immersed more of myself into the expansion of this company, leaving little time to develop my own.

Just like the night driving and viewing from the backseat can lull someone to sleep, I fell asleep on my life. Don't get me wrong; we achieved many successes. However, I did not feel fulfilled. This is a pivotal lesson, don't confuse achievement or success with living on purpose. It began to become increasingly difficult. For every major milestone achieved, a major challenge followed. It seemed as if I was moving a boulder uphill. Many would have thrown in the towel. Maybe I should have at that point, but I was too determined not to let the challenges defeat me. As I discovered my purpose, I also discovered how God had wired me and how I was conditioned growing up. I am naturally driven; typically, I do not back down from a challenge. I remember Dad inspiring me, "you can do whatever you put your mind to." If something is difficult, I dig in deep. This may be to a fault because there are times when you need to walk away. How do you know when you are taking a back seat on your purpose? A tell-tale sign is a constant frustration. When you are walking in your purpose or the driver's seat, you have a sense of peace. You are satisfied with yourself and content with where you are heading. When you are in the driver's seat of your purpose, you also have balance and appreciate the present. Well, I was not satisfied nor content. I spent many of my days building this enterprise and had forsaken my own, did not spend as much time with my loved ones who I hold dear, and I focused so much on the future (one day...) I was not living in the moment.

I believe God loves us too much for us not to find that joy and peace that walking in our purpose provides. I am convinced, He allows certain situations to come and disrupt our pattern to get our attention and to move us toward purpose, just like the truck that navigated Dad to safety. God loves us too much to continue to drift in a direction He has never desired for us anyway. That is danger. If not for disruption at times, we would never change. Change propels us to grow. I learned of activities that took place that went against my values. So, after seven years, I felt I had been engulfed in a fog, like a pillow snuffing the real me out. Again, I already shared how I am wired, so I may have endured longer than I should have. As women, we have been conditioned to endure situations for far too long. We sacrifice ourselves for other person's happiness to our own detriment. God allowed me to "see" some things that changed the trajectory of my being there. That aha moment, when I realized my worth and value, was a wake-up call. I realized this was not the vision I had for my life, so I did not have to remain there. That was the most liberating feeling. "We walk away not because we want others to realize our worth and value, but because we finally realize our own" (Robert Tew, 2016). I was not living a purposeful life.

What do you do when you realize you are not living your life's purpose? First, recognize; second, you move toward your purpose. When I decided enough was enough and prepared to get out of the back seat was when everything started to align in my favor. "You never realized how thick your fog was until it lifted" (J.R. Ward, 2012).

It was not an easy transition. I had to battle my way toward my purpose... against my own fears, other distractions, and the lies and confusion that was hurled my way during the transition. I was determined. I could no longer take a back seat. I had already wasted enough time. I had to totally walk away and could not take anything that I have created nor receive any remuneration for my contributions to this enterprise. I was so wounded and, at times, felt like a failure when I left. However, I was motivated by my faith that when armed with doing the right thing and obedient in living out my purpose, God will make provisions for me and restore anything I perceived I might have lost. Who would've known moving toward my purpose would position me in an organization to help thousands of women business owners through one of the toughest periods of the ages, the COVID-19 pandemic?

Shawntay Dixon is a 20-year business development professional with experience as a business consultant, trainer, and director of entrepreneurship programs. She is currently a program manager of a U.S. Small Business Administration Women's Business Center, Shawntay's leadership accelerated business growth of over 1,000 business owners and led to recognition as Women's Business Center of Excellence by the United States Small Business Administration. As business expert associate faculty, Shawntay taught undergrad and MBA programs at University of Phoenix's School of Business. She established the consulting firm Precisely Done Enterprises, LLC in 2007 and is credited with the successful turnaround of a 30-year healthcare company she co-owned and managed.

Shawntay holds an M.B.A. in Management, the Certified Workforce Development Professional designation, and is a Certified DISC Consultant. A continuous learner, she finds great joy in sharing her knowledge to elevate others. Shawntay is wife to Sam, mother to Shyanne and Jakari, and dog-mom to her beloved Twix.

Live Up to Your naME

Reshounn "Sun" Foster

Prologue

Welcome to a journal ride of journal writes of my Life's Calling. What I am called and what I am called to do have been a lifelong journey that's literally spelled out and encoded my name. I just didn't see it until I gave birth to a "Pure Spirit." How I was called to explore my naME came during the peak of what I named my Biblical Job Moment.

A severe series of family losses paired with joblessness, home foreclosure, finances, confusion, dread, and worthlessness showed me why Grandaddy Tom urged me to read the Book of Job. It wasn't until my Biblical Job Moment that I had come to personally understand longsuffering.

When suicidal ideations haunted me, I re-imagined "depression." I went from wailing to wordsmithing. I began re-designing my melancholy mental spaces with regenerative words that resonated with me. I renamed the state of depression my Womb State. Substituting darkness for divinity, time spent in isolation was used constructively for reflection, clarity, and wisdom from the ancestral realm. Anchoring my Self in the Womb State, journal writing quieted the inner chattering that comes with grief/loss and PTSD. Journaling is my psychotropic.

Journals are my playgrounds. A creative space for my "writes,' which are unedited streams of consciousness writing, prose, spirit writing, scripture, brainstorms, and memories. These writes I share are my sacred texts and based on the International Celebrate Your Name Week. Established by *onomatologist Jerry Hill in 1997, every day of the first full week of March has a theme to act on.

I dedicate these writes to my mother, Brenda (Firebrand), who told me early on, "Who you are is God's gift to you. Who you become is your gift to God." I write in honor of my daughter and namesake, Arian Reshounn, my eternal light and love. I uplift the name of my spiritual advisor Linda "Amina" Johnson, author of the *African Medicine Wheel*, who showed me what medicine I bring to this world and told me to "Write about the names." And to the Divine One whose whispers echo when I'm feeling lost or troubled, "Reshounn, live up to your naME."

*a person who studies etymology, history, fun facts, and the use of proper names.

Journal Write 1: Unique Name Day
Google your name.

Spirit whispers this at 4ish am. I am jolted from my sleep. A quickening is happening in my body, simulating a kaleidoscope of butterflies. I immediately respond to The Call to perform a vanity search. I begin re-memorizing John 1:1. Spirit-led, I write:

In the beginning was the Word and the Word was with God...and the Word was God...and the Word was made flesh...and you are flesh right now...and you are called by a word...your name...your name is a Word...the Word is capitalized as are all proper nouns...nouns are names of...people...and when asked your name, you answer, "I Am..." which is the name of God...when lost...in the darkness of Life...in the darkness of rough waters...call on The Word...The Name...call on your Self, too, for your own strength...when you are called...Have faith in your Self...the God in you...have faith that "I Am..." will answer your prayers in The Name...

Reaching through the darkness, I pat my bed until I find my smartphone. I press its button and see the light. I am lead through the portal of limitless information. I spell "R-e-s-h-o-un-n" in the search box and prepare for what of my Self will appear. My search yields a shortlist of results. I see my bolded name in one of the 1997 Adweek Volume 38 issues. I am credited as a copywriter for Kmart Corporation TV ads. At Don Coleman Advertising, I also wrote campaign ads for Carson Products, makers of Dark & Lovely no-lye hair relaxer, General Mills, and DaimlerChrysler. I didn't even know what a copywriter was when I applied. I was an English major and taught myself what I needed to get hired. I learned on the job how to write ad campaigns. I spell "R-e-s-h-o-un-n" in the search box.

Reshounn has no meaning. I key in July 22, 1968, and am amused by what pops up. I was born on Feast Day of St. Mary Magdalene. I share my birthday with history makers Alex

Trebek, George Clinton, Danny Glover… and my astro twin is the Virginia Slim ad campaign! Broadcast through the airwaves the day I was born was

"You've come a long way."

The VS ad was a game-changer for girls and women. Already a descendant of the Great Migration, the Civil Rights Movement, and the Women's Rights Movement, discovering this makes my entire life make even more sense. I've been navigating the frontiers of women's social justice issues. Women's sexuality, single motherhood, women in the workplaces, birth control, abortion…all the Isms; I am a living social justice moveMEnt!

Less than two decades after my mother birthed me, she performed the role of District Manager for Philip Morris International, makers of Virginia Slims. In high school, I had every Virginia Slims promo t-shirt, keychain, and Book of Days calendar. Unknowingly, mom and I had been fully immersed in our destiny. Less than two decades after that, I performed the role of copywriter for Don Coleman Advertising, writing ad campaigns. Coincidence or destiny?

I spell "R-e-s-h-o-un-n" in the search box. Reshounn has no meaning. I craft my own MEaning. I am Re, a pre-fix always beginning to start anew, always coming back like the sun. I am Shounn, which sounds like in Shine. I have learned Shounn is a variation of Sean, a derivative of John, like the forerunner to Jesus. The Light before The Light, which means "Jehovah has been Gracious." I am La Nise, Bright Goddess of Light. I am from the House of Porter, Gatekeeper, and Keyholder. I am from the House of Foster, Cultivator, and Promoter. I am from the House of Childs, The Protector of Youth. I am from the Houses of Berlerson, Donaldson, Hooper, Owens, Francis... I am from Detroit... America, with roots extending to Africa, England, and Scotland.

Why is Spirit calling me now in 2014? Is this an anointing, revealed 45 years after bathing in my mother's womb? Is this Spirit calling me to do what I'm called?

Journal Write 2: Discover What Your Name Means Day

Of the many birthday blessings I've received thus far, this one below ranks high. Only July 22, 2016, I asked a Jewish woman about the significance of my name beginning with "Resh," the Hebrew letter "r." I received her reply this morning with a birthday greeting:

The Ancient picture for this letter is [picture], the head of a man. This letter has the meanings of "head" and "man" as well as "chief," "top," "beginning" and "first," each of which are the "head" of something, as well as 'evil' or the 'potential for evil', and lastly, 'the poor'. The different meanings have to do with the many ways to spell 'resh' in Hebrew. Resh-yud-shin or resh-shin. So, it is a word that contains a paradox. The sages say that all beginnings or first things or leaders can be for good or for ill, for riches and bounty or for lack and poverty. The entire spectrum of possibility exists in everything new. So, to be a 'head' or a leader, to truly begin, is to become so humble, so poor (unattached in an ego sense from gain or outcome) that one can make room to address whatever one confronts in a very present manner... To be named Rosh or Reisha or Reshounn is

61

to carry the sense of humble leadership, willingness to begin, again and again, and to be conscious of the possibility of the good or not so good results of our decisions and actions.

I've been researching scriptures, readings, study guides and lecture videos, and contemplated what this means, i.e., I've been in my head about it. It's just fascinating to me what more is revealed and how one's name is so prophetic. My life has been a whirlwind of starts and stops. Forever creating new things, Always facing new challenges, Always changing job positions, catalyzing, inspiring, leading others to see things differently, etc. Whatever the change and challenge, I choose GOoD and use my powers for GOoD. I received this lettered confirmation today and look forward to a long prosperous life of Love and being a change agent wherever I go and with whatever I do —decisions made intentionally for The Greater Good.

ר Resh Psalm 119:153-160 NIV

> *[153] Look on my suffering and deliver me, for I have not forgotten your law. [154] Defend my cause and redeem me; preserve my life according to your promise. [155] Salvation is far from the wicked, for they do not seek out your decrees. [156] Your compassion, LORD, is great; preserve my life according to your laws. [157] Many are the foes who persecute me, but I have not turned from your statutes. [158] I look on the faithless with loathing, for they do not obey your word. [159] See how I love your precepts; preserve my life, LORD, in accordance with your love. [160] All your words are true.*

Journal Write 3: Happy Name Tag Day

My first name has eight letters, which takes up too much space on name tags. This is not good for the environment due to crumpling and trashing two or more tags per event because of underestimating the space to write R-e-s-h-o-u-n-n. I make the "Re" too big. The "sh" too small. I have to make sure the "o" and "u" have enough room. Otherwise, it looks like "au" and gets transcribed as such. Then I have to backtrack and request a correction. By the time I get to the edge of the tag, I have to squeeze in the "nn" and make them distinctly not look like an "m." Name tags are for conformists. I'd rather say my name. When we greet, their faces light up with happy-ness. "That's a pretty name," they say.

I'm happy to have a name that sounds pretty.

Sunshine also has eight letters and to flower childish for me to put on a name tag. Sunshine also the name of my name variant Rochon, Lela's character in Harlem Nights. I'm watchful of men's sly grins when they call me "Sunshine." I give them The Look and tell them, 'You don't know me like that.'

One day in the spring of 2012, I played hooky from work to attend the Enterprise Health Fellowship info meeting. Registering on-site, there wasn't a neatly typed name tag waiting for me to pin. Per usual, I screwed up "Reshounn" and had to write my name again and again. In the space of about 100 strangers, having a name that doesn't sound like it's spelled wasn't calming me down. I had to find a way to lighten up.

So, for fun, easy reading, and waste prevention, I decided to simply write "Sun" and introduced myself as such. Good God, I'm glad I did! I had truly witnessed that day the power of names. When writing "Foster Sun" into a spreadsheet, my great friend and Queen Sister Halima pointed out that my name means one who inspires warmth, joy, playfulness, and peace. She is the one who also saw "sun" embedded in my name.

Journal Write 4: Fun Facts About Names Day

I've been an anagrammatist since age seven. We create words using letters in a word. The words can become affirmation or reveal prophetic messages. For example, this is a prophecy with words encoded in my name: Reshounn is here to heal thru the lit arts.

Epilogue

If I can drive home one main idea, it is to tell you that reflecting on your name's meaning will anchor you as your destiny unfolds. You can move forward with stronger determination when you Live up to your naME.

Reshounn [Resh, Hebrew for "rabbi" + ounn rearranged spells "noun."] 1. Spiritual advisor of names 2. Sun/shine 3. B.A. English, Wayne State University. American Name Society Member.

A lifelong name enthusiast, transmedia storyteller, and multi-genre writer, Reshounn "Sun" Foster began her Self-study in 1991 when naming her daughter Arian. Research and introspection sparked The naME Project, artistic experiences based on anthroponymy—the study of personal names—including pop-up salons, author talks, therapeutic journaling, and wordplay. She inspires every individual she meets to research what they're called to clarify their "calling."

Sun performed "How My Daughter Got Her naME" in the inaugural storytelling production Listen to Your Mother – Detroit. Award-winning podcaster/writer Sarah Werner featured her on Coffee Break 009: reShoUNn. She also appears in the

"Urban Biographies: Ancient and Modern" online exhibit at the University of Michigan's Kelsey Museum of Archaeology.

Explore Your naME, www.reshounn.com.

From Insignificance to a Vibrant Life

Michelle G. Francis

Have you ever been in a place, and you felt powerless, not heard, inconsequential or invisible? I can recall in my early stages of growing up; I would strive to be seen, appreciated, or accepted by others. My attempts seemed fruitless. Regardless of my best efforts, it was never good enough. In many instances, I was made to feel stupid or verbally attacked. After all of that, I would feel emotionally assaulted and drained. How much can a person take? This feeling I am referring to is much more than being frustrated – it is more like I felt violated. Am I the only one feeling this way?

All the trauma and drama I experienced as I grew into adulthood, caused me to be a 'perfectionist' to compensate for the dreadful feeling of being insignificant. I was determined that those negative words rehearsed in my head would never be true in my life, so I always strived for perfection. I tried and kept trying to be perfect because I wanted to prove to them and perhaps myself that I was valuable. Trust me, that takes a lot of energy to keep this up.

I realized that I was in a crazy race of proving myself and this ultimately led me to the keeping up with the Jones' syndrome causing me to work 80 hours or more per week! I committed to and accepted every task on my job. It soon felt like I was the "yes" lady at my organization. Why? Because I was again proving I could do whatever was asked of me, and I could do it exceptionally well. I have a confession, during this period in my life, I was an ordained minister. I knew I was doing the work of the Lord and going beyond my ministerial duties to please the people I was serving. However, I was so "busy" doing the ministry that I was not actually pulling away to BE with the Lord, who loved me more than I loved myself.

As life would have it, as I was busy with life, out of nowhere, 'IT' happened. Yes, it was 'IT.' I was walking down the hall to one of my client's office and woke up in the hospital. The doctor informed me that I had a primary immune disorder, and I was severely dehydrated. In addition, the doctor informed me that if I had not come in when I did, I could have possibly perished. Although this could have been considered awful, it saved my life. I had to stop and ask myself, "why am I doing what I am doing?" This forced me to take a deep dive evaluation of myself.

Many times, in our family, job, and cultural dynamics, we may feel insignificant, and people will tell you how you should feel or what you should do without considering your thoughts, voice, or feelings. In 2020, our nation observed the voices of many cultures and people being marginalized, negatively stereotyped, and ignored. This can occur at your place of employment, church, and various organizations whereby someone will change or re-route your job, position, or responsibilities without communication with you and then wonder why the excitement you once had when you started the position has vanished because you are tired of asserting, proving, or making people see your value. Lastly, this can manifest by us trying to portray that we have a million dollars; however, we have more debt than assets and one paycheck away from being homeless.

I believe a shifting point must occur in our life when we realize our worth, identity, and value, whether received or not, loved or not, appreciated or not, is important!! At this critical point, we understand our identity, purpose, and assignment on this earth. At this point, we can SOAR no matter what. We realize that our assignment is greater than the opinion and views of men.

As stated above, I had to take a deep evaluation of my life and why I felt like I had to be the best at all things and failing terribly. First, let us look at the word "insignificant." Webster states it means "unimportant, trifling, inconsequential, a person without power or influence." As I was in the hospital for a week, I began to assess my life, and the Lord brought me to Isaiah 6:3-8 (Amplified Bible), which states:

> *"3 And one called out to another, saying, "Holy, Holy, Holy is the LORD of hosts.*
> *The whole earth is filled with His glory." 4 And the foundations of the thresholds trembled at the voice of him who called out, and the temple was filling with smoke. 5 Then I said,*
> *"Woe is me! For I am ruined,*
> *Because I am a man of [ceremonially] unclean lips,*

And I live among a people of unclean lips.
For my eyes have seen the King, the LORD of
hosts."

6Then one of the seraphim flew to me with a
burning coal in his hand, which he had taken
from the altar with tongs. 7He touched my mouth
with it and said, "Listen carefully, this has
touched your lips; your wickedness [your sin,
your injustice, your wrongdoing] is taken away
and your sin atoned for and forgiven."

8Then I heard the voice of the Lord, saying,
"Whom shall I send, and who will go for Us?"
Then I said, "Here am I. Send me!"

When I started reading this, all I could do is cry because I know
there is about to be a major shift, healing, deliverance, or
redirection in my life. During these seasons, I am always
brought back to the above passages, to the point I have called
these periods "Isaiah Moments."

Like Isaiah, I had to do a self-analysis and confront why I felt
insignificant and what was the root of it. I started meditating and
began to see periods of my childhood to adulthood where I
experienced traumas, hurts, negative words, and situations that
occurred, causing feelings of insecurity, rejection, abandonment,
and the need to be validated by men. These feelings put me in a
place of wanting to prove "THEM" wrong to my hurt and
demise. In addition, I had to take inventory of the people that
were around me. As I observed, I realized the people I associated
with were perfectionists as well. They had to prove something to

someone or somebody, not realizing that a person cannot put them in heaven or hell. I find we are sometimes so busy striving to be number one that it may result in unhealthy competition, envy, jealousy, and everything that goes with it. In addition, I took into account my healthy relationships and how they lived their lives. They were not trying to prove anything to anybody. They just wanted to glorify God and be the best version of themselves. They did not have time to be hating on anyone. Their focus was improving themselves daily, focusing on God, serving, and empowering others to do the same. These were the friends that helped me walk through the process and release myself from the negative words in my head.

The steps I took to move from stinking thinking and loving myself to the point where I accepted the good, bad, and ugly of me and still love me without the validation or acceptance of anyone else was not easy, but it was necessary for my healing and my life. I will share some of these steps with you; however, your process may be different. In addition, you may need someone to assist you as you walk through your own process.

Step 1: Forgive Yourself and Forgive Others

For me to move forward, I had to forgive myself for striving to make things happen to keep up with other people instead of totally trusting the Lord. I had to release the need of being accepted by men. In addition, I had to forgive the hurt, trauma, and pain caused by others in my life because it was keeping me in a cage and a vicious cycle of pain. Although those individuals may never say sorry or admit what they did, I had to release them and move on so I could be FREE.

Step 2: Release toxic relationships and environments

I had to take inventory of the relationships and associations around me. Do these people empower me to grow and BE the women that God called me to be? If the connections in your life put you in a place of unhealthy competition whereby you hurt others to succeed and bring out the worst in you, you should consider separating yourself from that person or environment. This may be an employer, organization, or group that makes you move from your own moral compass and cause ugly traits to arise in you.

Step 3: Positive Self Talk, Confident Communication, and Positive Relationships

I had to speak over myself who I am in God. For instance, I am victorious. I am the head and not the tail. I am the Lord's beloved. In addition, I listened to songs that spoke to who I am in God and how much the Lord loves me. This allowed me to love myself more and more. I had to do things to celebrate myself, whether someone else did or not.

Then I had to evaluate how I communicated with others and how I presented myself. Did I speak with knowledge and confidence regarding subject matters that I was an expert in, or did I speak with a question mark? I noticed when I dumbed down my ability and gifts that God placed in me; it put me in a place of powerlessness. I could not get mad at anyone because I was diminishing God's investment in me so others would not feel uncomfortable or intimidated. However, I was miserable. I want to caution you; some people will want to make you feel insignificant because they want to feel better. They will be "sweet-nasty" to you or say things to make you feel less than, so they feel greater. The sad thing is that people who do that have insecurities they are dealing with, and in those situations, we need to keep it moving to avoid the distraction and pray for them. Regardless of the scenario, do not diminish who you are because the world needs you to BE all you have been destined to BE. Lastly, I had to shift my relationships and connect with EAGLE's and not with chickens.

Step 4: Solidifying my identity in Christ and Accepting ME

As I did in step 3, I was solidifying my identity in Christ. This was liberating because I began to surrender all to the Lord and be who He called me to BE without apology.

Many of us go through crossroads where we must reintroduce ourselves because many people see us in our past and do not see us in our present. In some situations, we have drawn back and made ourselves powerless. No matter the scenario, know that each day we are evolving, and some people will not change their view of you, and that is OK.

I encourage you to BE the woman of God and the man of God that the Lord has ordained you to be. Rise up and dream again. Rise up and love again. Rise up and let past hurts go. Rise up and LIVE the vibrant, exuberant, lovely, and fabulous life you are destined to live. I pray that this chapter will encourage you to reintroduce yourself from insignificance to a vibrant life.

Michelle Francis is a graduate of the RHEMA Bible Training Center in Tulsa, Oklahoma. She also has her Master's in Public Administration from American University with a focus on International Government and Not-for-Profit Consulting. Throughout her life, she has advised, trained, and empowered men and women who have experienced physical and emotional abuse, as well as individuals dealing with addictive behaviors. She is a voice of wisdom to the overwhelmed caregiver and the person that has been confronted with a terminal diagnosis. These life issues are dear to her heart because she has had to walk through all these traumas and trust God to keep her mind focused during the process. She has realized every betrayal, negative diagnosis, rejection, and fear was not just a trial to tear her down, but to fortify, build and expand her influence and territory to be a mouthpiece of healing for others to DREAM AGAIN and live their BEST LIFE.

How Bad Do You Want To Be Good? Finding Peace and Purpose

Toni Marie Henderson

Today as I write, I am a work in progress. I often reflect over my life and how I have often felt misunderstood, out of place, and left behind. I felt left behind in not being married, missed business opportunities, and the idea of the so-called "American Dream." Over the years, I have overcome many battles: mental, spiritual, financial, and loss —the loss of family members and the loss of a friend due to suicide of which I witnessed.

I was born in California to two Detroit-born parents, Marvin and Sharon. They are two of the hardest working, driven people that I know. They are huge motivators for me and are a big part of my life. Throughout the years, I have been blessed with a huge blended and extended family that includes step-mothers, step-fathers, brothers, sisters, and a host of nieces and nephews.

As a child, I always loved television and movies. I still do, in fact. Television and movies were my escape as an only child. I really wanted to be an actress and go to California. I was mildly obsessed with the thought of being on TV and in movies. It made me happy. It was my comfort zone and space.

Overall, my childhood was happy. I never wanted for anything. I ate well; we always had a home; I had clothes, toys, and whatever else I needed. I was a good kid. I talked to myself a lot, being an only child. My toys and inanimate objects became my friends, and I was often in a world all by myself.

I did well in school and had friends. My family on both sides was close. We had regular get-togethers, social and holiday gatherings. I loved spending time with my cousins and grandparents.

As an adult, I wonder about some of the challenges and traumas that plagued me. What contributed to my self-sabotage? Was it my parent's divorce? How did I see men overall? What made me choose men that led to unhealthy relationships? What was I afraid of? Why didn't I feel confident and worthy like my parents? How did I end up here? What happened to me?

My parents are self-driven, aggressive, successful people. I have a degree in Spanish. Why am I not using it? Why didn't I become a veterinarian? Why am I not married? How did I end up on welfare and in Section 8 housing? Why didn't I pay my bills on time? How and why did I ruin my credit? How did becoming a parent change me? What would my life have been like? Was I depressed and traumatized and didn't even know it? My answer is yes.

We all experience some type of trauma: domestic, familial, abuse. Marriages and divorces have stress. Families have stress. Friendships have stress. Relationships have stress. We have all experienced these in our lifetime. I do not think that we fully understand or believe how stress and trauma really affect us.

During my young adult years, I lost myself due to a lot of stress from expecting to do well in life.

After high school, I was suddenly an adult and making adult decisions that I clearly did not understand.

College became another world with its responsibilities. Suddenly I was responsible for earning my own money and taking care of myself. I accumulated bills and credit card debt. I had debt in collections and negative bank accounts. I had anxiety and felt like I was drowning.

Then, I became a mother. Another role that I was not ready for. I will never claim to be Mother of the Year, but I truly love my son Omari with all of my heart. I would certainly do a lot of things differently if I could, but I can honestly say that I did the best that I could at the time.

As women, we lose ourselves in the identities that society and cultures place on us. We feel like we have to be the perfect mother, be the perfect weight, marry the perfect man and have the perfect life with no cares or financial worries.

I would often compare myself to others and wonder where I went wrong. I focused on what I perceived as success: the money, houses, cars, vacations, etc. While those things are important, I had to find peace from within.

I would feel so low and feel like a failure. I would try many things to be better. I wanted to be better. But I never felt like I got anywhere. I felt like everything that I tried produced minimal results. I felt hopeless. My inside joke to myself was: "If I'd done things right, I would have been married and divorced at least twice by now" (laugh). I know that my family worried and wondered about me at times.

I had to learn to accept accountability, learn to listen, and be patient. I had to learn to stop comparing myself to others and to stop blaming others. I had to learn to pay my bills on time, to "stop the bleeding," and stop sabotaging myself in all aspects of life.

The main thing is that I WANTED to change. I began to change my thinking. I stopped being angry and defensive. I began to hold myself accountable. I stopped being mad at everyone and blaming outside circumstances. I began to feel better about myself. Going to church helped a lot with my mindset. I credit Life Renewal Church of Farmington Hills, Michigan. I thank Pastors Vicky and Glen Love for their leadership.

Jim, who is close and dear to me, helped me understand that there are many sides to a story; that there are many points of view. We talked about how we do not always know everything to create a judgment. I only saw things from my point of view. I was the "victim."

It always seemed to me that it was easier for others to get ahead, to build their businesses and dreams. They had each other. They had their own team and clique. They had the support, the know-how, and the money. I know that there is a lot more to it than that. I also know that it's not that easy and simple. I was hurt and disappointed; that's how it appeared to me at the time.

I was always a team player. I wanted to excel. I followed the rules. I was friendly, reliable, punctual, and dependable. I was excited and eager to see where the business was going. I anticipated being a part of the growth. I had hoped and anticipated that I would grow as well: experience, title/promotion, money. I grew tired and disappointed time and time again over the years when that ended up not being the case. I would input thoughts and ideas and see my ideas being used but not get the credit or money. This kept happening to me over the years at various places I worked. I felt defeated like I couldn't get ahead no matter how hard I tried. You feel like a failure when you haven't "made it" by a certain age.

During these years, I was saddened and frustrated. I couldn't find my place in the workforce. I couldn't find the right man and have a healthy relationship. My son had ADD, and we now know, he was bipolar. His suffering could have been handled differently. I was emotionally and financially depleted. I was getting it from all sides.

It took years for me to understand that I had more growing to do mentally, skill-wise, and attitude-wise.

What I have learned is that nobody owes you anything. Prayer and hard work go hand in hand. I also realized that it simply wasn't my time. I was better than how I was living, and I knew it.

I focused my time and energy on myself and created my own lane. One of the greatest things that I learned from my parents and my gym "family," is Group Fitness Instruction. Being a Group Fitness Instructor teaches leadership, communication, confidence, organization, structure, time-management, multi-tasking, and many other skills.

These are the same skills that I use to run my own business and brand, Tone It Up! Fitness. I have become my own boss. I have purpose and long-lasting friendships and bonds that I am very grateful for.

I am learning to step into my leadership and greatness. I have found my purpose and am working to achieve my goals. I use the term step into my greatness from singer and songwriter Neyo. He advised a contestant on the World of Dance television competition to "step into his greatness" as a dancer. That quote stuck with me because it was strong, purposeful, and powerful.

It took me getting sick and tired of being sick and tired to begin my journey for positive and healthy change.

I take care of business now. My daily motto is "let me do it now before I don't." I had to learn to stop procrastinating and to be patient while learning. I am doing things and activities that are exciting, challenging, and out of my comfort zone. I realize that I have more learning and growing ahead. I am not where I want to be, but I am happy to know where I am headed. What I thought were mistakes and failures in the past were actual skills and experiences needed to place me where I am today.

My dad and I had many heart-to-heart talks. We talked about how time catches up with you faster than you know. We talked about the discipline of staying in shape and how that discipline leads to discipline in life. One of his favorite songs is a country song by Tim McGraw called "How Bad Do You Want It" The song speaks of "hunger," drive, discipline, and determination. My dad asked, "How bad do you want to be good (in life)? We laughed at the irony of the question. He and his wife Deborah worked hard, stayed aggressive, and are now franchise owners of Anytime Fitness.

I have seen my mother work hard, still today, for everything she has: her own house, car, and material possessions. I see her drive, tenacity, and strength. I know of the many struggles that she has gone through personally and professionally. Sharp-witted and quick thinking, she came out on top. I envy her and am working to follow in her footsteps.

Today at 48, I can say with pride that I have excellent credit, my bills are paid on time, my bank accounts are positive, I am no longer on welfare, and I am not living in Section 8 housing. I have strong and healthy relationships with my family members. Our family get-togethers consist of the important things in life: food, drink, love, and laughter. I have confidence and purpose.

What I would like to stress is: once you decide to do better. You will be better. Your energy and focus will shift. Your life will change. You will know and understand that you have choices; and that you are in control. You will know your worth on both personal and professional levels. Finding peace and purpose is key in going forward with whatever you choose to do. It is an ongoing journey and process.

So, how bad do I want to be good? I'm still finding my "hunger," but I have come a long way, and I'm proud of that. Where I am today is on a good and positive journey.

Psalm 46:5: God is in the midst of her, she shall not be moved. (ESV)

Toni Marie Henderson is a mother of one son, Omari. She is also a Group Fitness Leader. She instructs low-impact group fitness classes of multiple genres and age levels. Sharing her "art" of group fitness, leading, and building life-long friendships is her passion. She can be seen leading classes live on Facebook through her Tone It Up! Fitness page as well as through Zoom. Toni enjoys music, dancing, reading, writing, and journaling. She also enjoys creating vision boards to help motivate and reach her goals. Toni has a bachelor's degree in Spanish Language and Literature from Oakland University in Rochester, Michigan. She is certified through the Athletics and Fitness Association of America (AFAA), The National Kidney Foundation of Michigan, and Schwinn Cycling Certification. Psalm 31: "She dresses herself with strength and makes her arms strong." Toni considers herself: "Destined To Win!"

Author's note: Photo credit: www.elaynegrossphotography.com 248-543-4090.

Awful to Awesome: Brown Girls Journey to Lead Technology

Dr. Tosha Padgett Johnson

Have you ever just sat back and thought about your life? Are there experiences in it that leave you in a state of awe? Do you ever wonder how you got to this place?

Depending on what is going on in your life at the moment, that state of awe can be a feeling of negativity or positivity. The best way to say it, you can be feeling awful or awesome about your situation.

Over the years, I have wondered how such a powerful feeling, such as being in AWE of something, could lend such a variance of emotions and feelings. I will admit, I have had my share of feeling both ways, but I sometimes feel that the awful feeling sneaks up on me more than ever when it relates to my career.

BEGINNING

Some people are born into a family with money. They know exactly what they are going to do when they grow up by looking at their parents. They know they are going to have a successful CAREER and not just work a job. Similar to an heir of a major company, their future is laid out for them.

For me, this was not necessarily the case. My parents were married, and I was their second child. My father was a Vietnam vet, and my mother started college but did not finish. My parents separated when I was 12 years old. My mother was a hard worker, and she had a job that allowed her to provide for my sisters and me. She worked with computers at a bank. So, I thought when I grow up; I am going to be like her (I guess I was my mother's heir). As I grew up, I realized we were not rich but were not poor.

When I went to high school, I learned that the technology field made you a lot of money. I liked computers, and I liked money! Those two things fit well with me. I made every effort to be the best student I could possibly be. I was at THE best college preparatory high school in Detroit, Cass Technical High School.

In the 1990s, the computer and technology industry was not a field that women typically went into. Most of the time, they felt that the only reason women should learn about computers was to become an Executive Secretary (now called Executive Administrative Assistant). Computers and technology are built of two different areas, software and hardware. For software development or data management, you need good mathematical and analytical skills. In hardware, you need to be good with your hands. Computers were extremely large back then, and I had no desire to learn the hardware side. I was interested in database management and programming.

As a high school senior, I received an internship. This was one of the first times that I felt great about my ability. I landed a PAID internship at one of the leading technology companies in the area. This was a guaranteed internship for every summer while I was in college with hopes to be hired on. I was feeling quite awesome!

There was an equal number of female and male interns. The females were interning in positions where it seemed to be more clerical work than technical work. The male interns were in positions where they were applying their coding or supporting hardware knowledge within the organization. My assignment was to file items in the company's technical library. I was extremely disappointed during the first year. At the end of summer evaluation, I brought the inequality to their attention, and the next year changes were made. I learned so much moving forward.

COLLEGE

Imagine growing up, going to school and everyone looked like you. You were at the top of your class and felt awesome about your education standing. Then imagine you are put into a situation where you are the minority. There is no one in your environment that looks like you, and your support system is gone. You have no cheerleader, and everyone is working against you. How do you think you can blossom and fulfill your dreams? This was me.

I stepped onto a college campus for the first time as a student. Being a first-generation college student, I felt like a fish out of water. I had no one I could talk to about anything. I had always been independent and self-sufficient, but this was the first time I really felt alone. This was a level of insecurity I had never before. I felt like all eyes were on me. No one in the classroom looked like me. I thought this was weird because I had just seen other black students in the student union, but why were none of them in this class with me?

I sat down for the Honors English class, and everyone in this class was white. When I came into the class, they looked at me like I had something on my face, or I smelled. One of the other students asked me if I knew what class this was? She acted like she wanted to make sure she was in the right classroom. I answered her and sat down. It did not hit me until the professor entered the room and he stared at me like me being in this class was out of the norm. In the mid-1990s, I guess this predominately white institution was not used to minorities placing high enough to be in such a course. I was in this course, and before I left, the professor would remember my name forever.

There was only one student that would talk to me in the class. She was from Canada and commuted to the University for class every day. She was always nice and being an honors English course; she thought I was extremely smart. I submitted my first assignment and received a B+. On the next assignment, I received the same grade with little feedback. My classmate could not believe I was not receiving an A. One assignment she asked if we could submit the same assignment because she did not believe I was being graded fairly. I was not for it, but she insisted, and I gave in. I was hoping our intuition was not true. I could not let this professor do this, but I also felt like why me. Why would I have to be the one to call this TENURED professor out? We submitted our identical papers with different names. She received an A++ with raving comments. I received a B+ with no comments at all.

This was awful. After consulting with the professor, he insisted that they were not the same and that I was causing problems. The student and I followed the proper channels to report him, and the tenured professor retired early.

This situation was awful for me but turned into an awesome situation for next the student that looked like me. It was a very difficult time for me because I still felt isolated at the school. In my technology classes, I was even more of a minority. In my computer programming course, I was the only female and the only African American. The odd thing was the other minority in the class was a Caucasian male. Everyone else was foreign to the United States.

Our professor assigned the class a semester-long group assignment to design a scientific calculator. It was worth 50% of our grade. No one wanted me to be in a group with them, even the other minority (Caucasian male). They were not polite in telling me that they didn't want to partner with me because I was a woman. Once I spoke to my professor, a Caucasian male, he said, "Do it by yourself. You do not need a group." I was furious! Isn't it his job to make the students work in a group!!! What is he doing?!

I spent so much time in the computer lab working on this one project during that semester. I was doing the work of four people. I had no computer at home, so I stayed in the campus lab. I spent many nights driving home with my eyes were full of tears. I felt like how I was being treated was so unfair. I was mad at my classmates. I was mad at my professor. I was mad at the world for making me DIFFERENT!!!

As we got closer to finals and were working in the lab, I noticed a couple of my classmates looking at me while working on their project. One of my classmates looked at me and then looked at his group partner, smiled, and said, "I know we will do better than at least one group," followed with a laugh. I was now even more DETERMINED!!! I was going to finish this project and fulfill all the requirements.

The final presentation day came, and it was time to present. I raised my hand to go first. I was exhausted from staying up late for the last two weeks. After presenting, my classmates were completely shocked. They looked amazed and confused. I soon realized my project was the only one that was completed. The professor stood up and gave me praise.

When taking the next class in this series, I was with most of the same classmates and the same professor from last semester. Another group project was assigned, but you would have thought I was Bill Gates because everyone wanted to partner with me. My professor looked at me with a smirk on his face; he politely said, "Ms. Padgett, it is proven that you are capable of doing this by yourself, but you need to make sure you can work with individuals that have lower skill level than you. You will run up against this a lot when you graduate." I smiled back at him and chose the best two individuals to work with me. That was my first taste of project managing a team.

CAREER

The experiences in college equipped me for my work environment. I was never turned down from a job because of a lack of experience, education, or personality. My resume reflected a very well-rounded and experienced Information

Technology (IT) professional, overqualified for some jobs. Unfortunately, I am not a white man. I am not a foreign man. I am not a MAN, but I AM black! It bothered me that they saw no fault in discriminating against me just because of my look!!!

The determination to succeed never left me. The rejection made me stronger and taught me to make myself versatile in the technology industry. Previously, I never wanted to learn anything about the hardware side of the industry, but now I can set up a network, fix a computer and program the application to run on that computer by myself.

The push back from my employees, peers, and management does not come just because of my skin color, but it also comes because I am a woman. You have to deal with racist and male chauvinist many times when managing technology. These adversities did not prevent me from earning my MBA in Technology and a Doctorate in Management. I never wanted to be rejected because of a lack of education or experience.

One incident made me realize that I had arrived, and my skillset was not being ignored. In one of my past places of employment, I had been the Director of Technology and was working as Interim Vice President of Technology. While I did the job and did it well, the organization still had the position posted as they searched to fill it. Instead of hiring me, the organization decided to change the position to Chief Information Officer and hired a Caucasian male from the outside instead. I did not stay at the organization much longer after that, even though I had developed a very strong IT team. After leaving, I receive a call from the leadership of the organization asking for my assistance.

I was flattered that they recognized my skillset, but I did not assist.

The biggest lessons I have learned through school and my career was that there will be moments that are awful but work through them because they are developing you to get to the awesome moments of life.

Dr. Tosha Padgett Johnson, a Detroit native, has over twenty-five years of experience within the technology industry. She is currently an Executive Manager over Technology for Canton Township. Dr. Johnson is a professor at Northwood University and a part-time Assistant Professor at North Central University. Her education began in Detroit Public Schools, and she is a graduate of Cass Technical High School. Dr. Johnson graduated from Wayne State University with a bachelor's degree in Information Systems Management, Oakland University with an MBA in Management Information Systems, and Colorado Technical University with a Doctorate in Executive Leadership Management.

Dr. Johnson is widely known and respected for her dedication to community service. She has a passion for mentoring youth and working in her community. She believes in giving back, so she created the Dr. Tosha Padgett scholarship fund for undergraduate women pursuing degrees in Science, Technology, or Business. While she has held various leadership positions in non-profit organizations and received numerous awards for her philanthropy, her pride and joy will always be her two daughters.

Against All Odds

Sherita Jolly

For many years, I avoided telling my story. I worried about being judged; I felt ashamed and embarrassed. Honestly, I didn't want people to know about my mess. I didn't want to appear weak or vulnerable. I learned a long time ago how to put on a happy face and appear strong regardless of how I was feeling, and I was good at it. I could be at my lowest point, and no one would ever know. Many wouldn't believe me if I told them because I always had a smile on my face. I appeared happy and full of joy, but that was rarely the case. It seemed like something would always come and steal my joy. I found myself constantly having to fight to get it and to keep it. I've heard everyone has a story, but everyone doesn't tell it. Today I'm telling mine, and hopefully, it will help someone.

I was born and raised on the West side of Detroit. I am the oldest of four children. I am my mother's firstborn child and my father's only child. Growing up, I didn't have the traditional family structure. My childhood was what some would call dysfunctional. No mom or dad to cook me dinner or tuck me in at night and give me kisses. Honestly, I had no structure at all. My parents were both teenagers when they had me. My mom was fifteen years old, and my dad was nineteen. My mother was young, beautiful, and smart with big dreams. Her future was bright. My dad was smart too. He was quite handsome and a charmer with a bright future as well. They were a young couple in love, headed in the right direction, but decisions were made that took them on another path and changed our lives forever.

Both of my parents became drug dealers and users. Drug addiction led to my childhood being unstable and full of chaos. My mom and dad separated, and it was just my mom and me for a while. Some of my childhood memories are vague, but some I'll never forget. I remember being outside playing with my friends when the police kicked our door down and took my mom and her friends away in handcuffs. I didn't really understand what was going on at the time, but I remember drugs and guns being removed from our home. All of the neighbors came outside and were watching and whispering. My friend's parents wouldn't allow them to come to my house and play anymore because my house was "the drug house." I believe this was the first time I felt embarrassed and ashamed of my mom. I was getting older and starting to understand. I continued to live with my mom off and on in between rehab stints and prison bids, but the last time she got arrested; I had to go and live with my maternal grandmother. My mom had gotten arrested; and this time it was serious, she was facing a lot of prison time, and they wouldn't let her out on bond.

Thankfully, my grandmother, Mama Jolly, was able to take me in and welcomed me with open arms. Mama raised me on the West side of Detroit. We lived in a little white house on Terry Street off Schoolcraft. I learned so much in that little white house. Mama taught me how to cook, clean and how to pray. Mama struggled to make ends meet, but she always found a way to keep a roof over our heads and food on the table. Some may call our neighborhood the ghetto or the hood, but it was home to me, and I was happy to be there. I didn't have to worry about moving from house to house anymore. Mama provided me with stability. Mama and her husband, my grandfather, bought that little house on Terry Street many years ago when they moved to Michigan from Tennessee. Mama wasn't going anywhere. She lived on Terry Street all of my life and most of my parent's life. That's where my mom and dad met. They were neighbors. I remember my grandmother telling me stories about how she tried to keep my mom away from my dad because she saw my mom heading down the wrong path, but my mom wouldn't listen to her. Mama said she was hardheaded and fast; that's how she ended up pregnant with me, and I better not follow in her footsteps. Mama was sweet and loving, but she spoke her mind and didn't hold any punches. Years passed, and I was still living on Terry Street with Mama. I was a teenager and found myself following in my mother's footsteps. I wasn't listening to Mama; I was hanging out with crowds that Mama disapproved of. We weren't using drugs, but some of my friends were selling them, and we definitely knew how to party. My cousin Taki and I were partying one day when she introduced me to Raphiele; he was tall with caramel skin and a beautiful smile. We exchanged numbers, went on a few dates, and made it official. He was my boyfriend, and I was his girlfriend. I was head over heels for him. We spent a lot of time together, and the next thing I knew, I was pregnant. How did I let this happen, and how was I going to tell Mama is all that kept running through my head? I was so afraid. My boyfriend didn't share the same emotion as I did. He was excited he was going to be a father. He said he wanted a daughter.

A few weeks passed, and I didn't have a choice but to tell Mama Jolly and my mom that I was pregnant. My grandmother's disappointment in me ripped my heart apart; all she wanted was for me to succeed and not end up being a statistic. How did I end up pregnant? After dealing with the emotions that came with telling Mama, I felt relief, but it didn't last long.

On Tuesday, October 5, 1993, I received a call from my cousin Taki. She was crying hysterically, and she said, "Raphiele's gone." What do you mean gone? "Someone shot him. He's dead." The pain I felt after hearing those words is indescribable. I wailed from the pit of my stomach. That day I felt a different kind of pain. It felt like someone had ripped a piece of my heart out of my chest. My heart was broken. Raphiele, my boyfriend and the father of my unborn child, was gone. He had been murdered. I felt like I was in a nightmare, and I couldn't wake up. I was seventeen years old, pregnant, and alone. I felt hopeless. I started thinking maybe the things people said about me were true; maybe I would end up being just another statistic. A young, black, single, teenage mom on welfare. Is that how my story was supposed to end? Was I going to be just another statistic?

After attending my boyfriend's funeral, I found myself spending a lot of time alone. I felt tired and physically drained all of the time. All I wanted to do was stay in bed and never leave. I stayed in bed a couple of days but eventually, I pulled myself together for my baby and I attended my doctor's appointments and school. It was my senior year in high school. This should've been a memorable time for me, but it wasn't. For the next several months, I barely functioned. I would attend class, go to doctor's appointments when needed, eat and sleep. I didn't find much pleasure in anything. I gained 60 pounds during my pregnancy. This wasn't good for my baby or me. After delivering her, I found myself unhappy with the way I looked, and I was depressed. It took a lot for me to say those words. Growing up, we didn't speak of depression or any form of mental illness.

I knew something was wrong, and I didn't like how I was feeling, so I did the only thing that I knew, and that was pray. I didn't have a close relationship with God, but I remember Mama telling me that I could talk to God about anything, so I did. I poured my heart out. I cried and cried on my hands and knees. I prayed, yelled, and I screamed. I questioned God. I wanted answers. I wanted to know why? Why was I born to parents addicted to drugs? Why was my unborn child's father murdered? Why did bad things keep happening to me? Why me? Doesn't everyone deserve to experience joy and happiness? Two parents to love, nurture and guide them? Why didn't I have that growing up? Why won't my little girl get to have both of her parents? As I reflect back, I realize I was angry with God. I was angry that I was born into a life filled with hurt and pain. I was angry that I was left to raise my daughter alone.

On Monday, March 14, 1994, my life changed forever. I became a mother to a beautiful baby girl, and I named her Rashiele. She was the cutest baby that I had ever seen. She was mine, and I was hers. I was responsible for another human being. Rashiele and I ended up living with Mama Jolly. Mama taught me how to care for her but honestly, taking care of her came naturally.

A few months passed, and I graduated from high school. I didn't really have plans after that, but I knew I wanted more. I was an adult now responsible for another person with decisions to be made. What was I going to do with my life? I decided to enroll in school and me and my baby girl went away to college. Education and college degrees aren't for everyone, but it was my way out, my way to a better life for me and my child. I wanted to be successful; failure was not an option. I turned all my hurt and pain towards finding ways to be great. I stopped feeling sorry for myself and developed a closer relationship with God. I talked to God regularly and learned to listen. My outlook on life changed. I was no longer asking God why me. I was thanking God for making me strong enough to endure. Everyone has a purpose in this world, and God allows things to happen to help shape you into who you are called to be so that you can fulfill that purpose. I searched for purpose in my pain, and I learned that happiness and joy are not dependent on my circumstances. Some may think that I'm successful because I have an amazing career, a profitable business, a beautiful home, and someone to share my life with. I'm successful because I'm finally happy, and my happiness isn't dependent on people, things, or circumstances. I have learned to find joy in the little things. Be grateful for everything because it could be worse.

Sherita Jolly is a Board-Certified Nurse Practitioner, entrepreneur, and mother of four. She is the founder of JannahsCollection.Com and NurseJolly.Com. Sherita has been an entrepreneur for nearly two decades and a nurse for 13 years.

Sherita is passionate about helping others and believes that Allah allows things to happen to you to shape you into who you are called to be. Sherita's journey has not been easy, and she believes by sharing her story, she can help others who may have experienced some of the same struggles. She completed her Master of Science in Nursing Degree at Spring Arbor University, Spring Arbor, Michigan, Bachelor of Science in Nursing Degree at Oakland University, Rochester, Michigan, and Bachelor of Business Administration Degree at William Tyndale College, Farmington, Michigan.

Visit her online at www.nursejolly.com
Sherita Jolly
470-223-8372
Sherita@nursejolly.com
www.nursejolly.com

www.jannahscollection.com
June 19th
4480 S. Cobb Dr. SE #497
Smyrna, Ga 30080

I Will Let Nothing Stop Me!
Min. Ruth King

It's been some years now, and I can't keep saying "widow"—"I am still grieving." Or can I? I refuse to use that as an excuse not to do what I am called to do.

We are now in a pandemic, and things have been changed for almost two years. In that time, I have not been back in my church. Looking back, I would not have missed a day of church. Even when my husband passed, I was in church the next day.

This pandemic has shown what's on the inside of me. Church IS NOT the building. Church is the people. I would always say, "people won't read the Bible; they read you!" This season has shown me that the Word of God is hidden in my heart. I also found out that I am an intercessor. Yes, I am a carrier of God's Word. I found out I can stand alone. Yes, it's nice to have people, but sometimes you have to go alone when people are not available to get the job done. In reality, you are not really alone; you have Jesus! There is an old hymn that reminds us, "If Jesus goes with me, I'll go anywhere!"

God has called me to encourage women, and He has called me to mentor children. God sends women to me, and I don't have to go looking for them. I don't look like what I've been through, which allows me to discuss unexpected topics. I am open and transparent about my story, and that is often helpful in getting people to open up. I also love children, and this is why I work in the school. I get a chance to love on them, providing the love many of them do not get at home. God created a platform for me, but I have not seen them during the pandemic. I miss them, and hopefully, they miss me too. Children keep us young with their energy and our minds sharp with their questions.

The devil sends people, situations, and obstacles to distract or stop you from focusing on what God has you doing or wants you to do.

When I decided to pray on Facebook Live, the devil became very busy. However, it was good to know that the people I worked with were listening in. Everyone needs prayer, whether you realize it or not. The Facebook Lives led me to prayer with a prayer group on Tuesdays. The devil didn't like that either. It didn't stop me. It motivated me, and I began to pray with two groups on Tuesday night. OMG! The devil was saying, "this is too much prayer." However, nothing was going to stop me. As I was praying one night with a family, they asked me if I get tired of praying, and I told them I could never turn down praying.

The constant praying has come with the devil sending distractions. My first distraction was with my health. Right before the pandemic, my doctor diagnosed me with diabetes. During the pandemic, the doctor could not get my blood pressure under control. Anytime your health is at risk, your mind is focused on trying to get better and NOT the things of God. But I must do what I was sent to do; therefore, I knew God would heal me, and He did. He healed me of diabetes. Although I am still working on my blood pressure by His stripes, I am healed of that also.

Now that I am sitting at home doing nothing, I feel like the devil is saying I am too old, but I am not hearing it! People are still finding me. The world is still in need of me, and I WILL LET NOTHING STOP ME!!!

Although heaven is our ultimate goal, our lives on earth are all about souls-- bringing them to Christ and allowing God to heal their heavy hearts. I have talked with people whose hearts are so heavy they don't think they can live. What do you mean you don't want to live? You are not the giver of life. So how can you just take a life?

Let's walk this thing out by praying, communicating with the Father. This means you have to stop and listen then read His Word. We are so blessed that we can listen to God's Word at any time. Don't forget to put on the WHOLE armor of God! This will shield you from the obstacles that can become distractions along your path to becoming who God has created you to be.

I want you to follow my lead. I love that old song, "Where He Leads Me I Will Follow," because it keeps me grounded and prevents me from going astray when life gets turbulent. Let God lead you, and don't let anything stop you from doing what you are called to do.

"Where He leads me, I will follow, I will go with Him all the way." This has been the battle cry and life theme for this widow, mother, grandmother, sister, spiritual mother, and mentor to many people young and seasoned in the church. Graduate of Ambassador Bible Training School, Southfield, MI. Minister Ruth King, licensed, Associate Minister of Triumph Church, was first appointed as the Ministry Leader of Decision Time Counselors (taking in souls for Christ) then appointed as the Administrator of Triumph University. Worked in the capacity of Teacher/Instructor and Presider. Now working in a non-profit organization as Executive Director and radio show host as well as working in the public schools as a secretary and mentor to 3rd and 4th grade girls.

She has been in church all of her life. Prayer and Praise is her lifestyle, her home is affectionately called "Prayer Headquarters." She recognizes that one of the greatest weapons against the devil is PRAYER & PRAISE; praising God in the midst of adversity and pain, knowing that God will give the Victory. She always says, "Praise God I don't look like what I've been through." Called also as an intercessor, she doesn't get much sleep and is running with the mantel of her mother who was also a great woman of faith. Min. Ruth recognizes that she's called to the nations and it's time to cry aloud and spare not!

Many doors have opened for her. She served as Choir Director for many years and has had the opportunity to teach and direct alongside some of Detroit's elite musicians. Her transparency during worship compels others to enter into the presence of God with humility and boldness. She's standing on the Word knowing that she will do "greater works" as the Word of God states. You will find that many people just walk up to her and start talking about their lives. She uses this as a tool to reach the lost and encourage those that feel alone. Min. Ruth is about the Father's Business, and she knows that her steps are ordered by the Lord.

She counts it an honor and privilege to minister to God's people; whether it's in song, an encouraging word, preaching and/or teaching the Word of God or prayer. She boldly proclaims "People, it's not enough to be talented, we need to be anointed! It's the anointing that destroys the yoke."

 She does not want to be labeled as a "widow." Just called her "Blessed!"

She had no idea God had called her to write. Therefore, she wrote a chapter in the book called, "Crystal Clear—Sisters Walking in Purpose with Clarity, Focus & Faith." She is very thankful for the door to write, again, has been opened.

ruthettaking@gmail.com

Destined to Soar

Dawn Nash Rutland

What happens when the perfect life you envisioned for yourself
falls apart? When the union of "'til death do us part" dissolves
through no fault or at the equal fault of both parties? What if in
the midst of the dissolution of the "tearing asunder" of both
parties who were one, but soon to be none, through their union
created a life with a purpose, whose purpose hung in the balance
between two worlds, between two people who thought that they
would be together forever, but inevitably would be apart?

Before I had my daughter, I could not have envisioned my life
with a child. In my mind, I had a list of places to which I would
travel and a proverbial "bucket list" of things to do and places to
see. I had no younger cousins growing up, so I had never
babysat anyone, not even a neighbor's child or my own siblings.
I actually gave birth later than my friends at the age of thirty-
one, which at that time was considered to have been later in life.

My pregnancy was far from traditional. I actually lost thirty
pounds during the pregnancy and vomited daily, needing
hospitalization for two weeks. I was only able to keep down
baby food and popsicles. In the hospital, they had virtually
exhausted every vein that I had in both arms. This meant that
they then had to use my ankle veins to insert a port to distribute

fluids to avoid further dehydration. Finally, I was released to go home after a few weeks.

With assistance from my husband at the time, and a port still in my ankle, and a pole with fluids that I carted from room to room in my two-bedroom apartment, I continued for another six weeks with bi-weekly home visits from a private duty nurse.

The six weeks concluded, and I returned to work. The situation began to take a turn for the better. I began the nesting process that most mothers go through in preparation to give birth. Continuing in my series of surprising events, I sprained my wrist and dislodged a filling during childbirth. However, it was all worth it. Th little person who would forever change my life emerged, making her entrance into the world. Any mother who has wanted a child can relate to this amazing and maybe scary feeling.

From the moment they cut the umbilical cord and place that precious new life on my chest, my first instinct was to love, shield, and protect this life with every fiber of your being and by any means necessary. The love between a mother and child is fierce and indescribable. In its purest sense, it robs you of the ability to be your once selfish and egocentric self because this little life who never asked to come into this world is now depending on you. Or, maybe you are an adoptive parent or relative who has made the conscious decision to devote yourself to raising a child or children as your own. Although you may not have given physical birth to this child or these children, you have equally committed to love, nurture, raise, and support another human being until adulthood, which is equally as strong as if you had given birth yourself. I named my daughter Jordan which means "The Descender." I believe that every child is named with an outcome in mind.

From a baby to a toddler, from a toddler to elementary school, time passed. I became a single mom while my daughter was three years old. I remember being referred to as a medium mom, meaning that I was sometimes strict and sometimes fun. To me, that meant that I was balanced, and that sounded like a reasonable parental description to me. Between the ages of five to seven, I distinctly recalled conversations between her and I that made me chuckle. "You're my sister, not my mom," to which I would lovingly and sometimes sternly reply that "No, I'm your mom."

Folks jokingly referred to my daughter as my shadow because everywhere you saw me, you saw her. She accompanied me ninety percent of the time when I wasn't working, and she wasn't at school or spending time with her dad. Before you know it, adolescence was upon us with the transition from middle school to high school. Participation in extra-curricular activities intensified, and preparation for the driver's permit, prom, and talk of post-high school planning.

It was going to be a very difficult transition for me to have my daughter leave home to attend college. Most parents shed tears during the graduation ceremony or as their child is in the process of packing to go away. Or maybe the tears fall as they are entering trade school, community college, or the four-year college campus for the first time. Sometimes the tears fall as you are pulling away from the campus, with their seat in the vehicle visibly empty. My tears actually began during her junior year as we began the serious financial and scholastic preparation. I wanted her to have the best chance of being accepted to college among her competition, and so I enrolled Jordan in a summer course during her junior year in high school. She had to wake up during the summer just like she would have done during any regular day during the school year. As I watched her walk to the bus stop, I remember her saying, "Thanks for ruining my summer, mom." I would cheerfully respond with a look and reply, "You're welcome."

Some days, I wouldn't even get to fully close the front door to the house before I let out an uncontrollable gut-wrenching sob which would go on for about ten minutes, leaving my eyes red and me dry heaving and exhausted as if my chest was giving up a lung. This went on for the four weeks that my daughter was in summer school. I had decided that it was best to let out the emotions rather than hold them in.. I was ecstatic about the possible opportunities for my daughter, but my heart knew that her absence would leave a void that I could not adequately voice, but my soul could already feel the impact of her impending absence. We had a home that I was so proud to have because I worked four jobs simultaneously at one point to afford the mortgage. Our home had two trees on either side, and one was near the door. This tree must have been full of birds. Sometimes I would become annoyed as they would fly by perching, chirping, zooming by the door, swooping, and almost colliding with me as I stepped out of the house.

One morning as I watched my daughter leave for the bus stop, I allowed myself to focus on something other than being sad and gave my attention to the sound of birds singing. I recognized that the sound was not at eye level but higher up in the tree. Deciding that I would see what was actually going on, I brought a chair from the inside of the house and positioned it against the tree, hoping that it would give me the height that I needed.

I stepped onto the chair and carefully separated the heavily leafed branches. What I saw was the most beautiful sight. There was a nest with exactly six perfect little chicks, otherwise known as hatchlings. Each had its head tilted with its beaks pointed upward. They were cooing and chirping, which I supposed was a signal to the absent mother bird that they were hungry. I realized that the mother bird would not appreciate the fact that I had uncovered her babies, and so I quickly let the branches close as if undisturbed and got down off of the chair before the mother bird returned. The next morning, I opened the door, and instead of being annoyed by the birds, I allowed my curiosity to get the better of me. I repeated the same process as the prior day, only this time I had my phone with the camera poised to capture a picture. I did not hear the mother, and I was able to capture a beautiful photo of the hatchlings. At this point, I had become preoccupied with the bird in the tree next to my door and her nestlings. I was told by a family friend who happened to be an avid bird watcher that usually the bird's nest for a few weeks until the mother weans them. At this point, I had become preoccupied with the activity of these chicks, giving daily attention to the comings and goings of the mother bird and her attention to her babies. This went on for a few weeks as I continued to shed my tears.

One by one, I would watch each fledgling emerge from the tree to soar into the air. It was an amazing sight. The chirping began to diminish, and I assumed that the fledglings were in the process of leaving the nest. One morning as I was listening and watching the tree, as what seemed like the last fledgling took flight. My heart was a little sad but still enraptured by the touching sight. A still small voice whispered to me, "You are the mother, and like the mother bird, you have nurtured your daughter from a hatchling to a nestling and now to a fledgling. You have prepared your daughter to soar!" "That is exactly what a fledgling is created to do." I felt tears uncontrollably well up in my eyes and throat yet again. The little chicks who were once a source of annoyance had spent weeks teaching me a valuable lesson.

I had prepared Jordan to soar, and now it was time for her to leave the nest. As a mother, I fulfilled my purpose in preparing her so that she could move on to go on to begin to fulfill her destiny away from the nest, otherwise known as home. Blessing after blessing was provided, and my daughter received a full-ride to include tuition, housing, and meals for a four-year undergraduate degree which she completed with honors. God's blessings continued, and she received a second full-ride which allowed her to complete her graduate degree, yet again with honors. Although my daughter was away for a total of nine years, she still returns to the nest to reconnect, refuel, and be refreshed before she takes flight to her next destination.

Educator, public speaker, and author Dawn Nash Rutland completed her undergraduate studies at LaSalle University with a bachelor's degree in English. She graduated with honors from George Mason University, with a Masters of New Professional Studies degree in Education. Her recognitions include but are not limited to: Teacher of the Year, USA Today All-Star Teacher Team, and Washington Post Woman of Distinction, She resides in the Washington, DC metropolitan area, where she has served in the educational sector and the classroom and community for more than 20 years. Her goal is always to celebrate, inform, and empower the reader. She has recently launched two books: The Early is Best College Quest and Hair-ish A 40- Day Nostalgic Hair Journal. You may contact her at dawnrutlandusa@aol.com for presentations and interactive seminars for community, educational, and corporate organizations.

On the Winning Team

Dr. K. Olivia Packer

For as long as I can remember, I've always set my sights on winning. I never wanted to be anything but first place. Of course, we know life doesn't work out that way. Besides, we can't grow until we face challenges in life. If someone were to ask me, I would say that it's in the challenges we face that we find out what winning really is. I would also tell you that it's important to be on a winning team.

What is a winning team?

There are a number of people on my team. I was one of those who was blessed to have winners in my "village" who had everything to do with who I am today. As a youth, I had grandmothers who took the time to pour into me. Their vision shaped me spiritually and mentally. I was also blessed with aunts who treated me like their own. But the individuals I want to talk about are affectionately called Mom and Daddy. They are the main players on my winning team.

I tell people I exist because of two inexperienced teenagers who heard harps playing and saw stars when they looked at each other. If you can remember that time in your life, think about the time you first fell in love and thought, "this is the one, and we'll be together forever." Well, the together forever part didn't happen exactly how they pictured it. But, I think they had the next best thing… ME! I believe having me started their journey to winning (experiencing challenge after challenge).

The odds were against the three of us from my conception. Most teenage parents become that statistic of people who get on state assistance for the rest of their lives, never making a contribution to society, and dying with someone passing a hat trying to bury them. Statistically, the offspring repeat the cycle. However, because of the women they were raised by (the best grandmothers on earth), they couldn't see having a child in high school as a death sentence to their dreams; it never crossed their minds. They still had a hunger for life and to make the most out of it; they still desired to "win."

The one thing I admire about them both is the fact that they never believed they ever fit the stereotype and were determined not to be a statistic. I watched them strive to be better on a daily basis and by any means necessary. There were a lot of things my father kept to himself until I was an adult. But, as for my mother, I watched her daily striving and pressing forward. I got the opportunity to watch a lot of her testimony unfold.

My mother is the youngest of my grandmother's two children and the only one to have children. My mother was the 'A' student throughout school and found school easy (like her mother, who graduated from high school early). I believe my grandmother saw the mirrored potential in my mother, and I wish she lived long enough to see some of those seeds planted in my mother sprout up and bloom. I know she would have been proud.

I watched in amazement how my mother would set goals, write them out, and execute them over and over again. Little did I know, at the time, that this would be the blueprint to how I engaged life and any goals I wanted to accomplish in life. Watching her sparked in me the notion that if I had a plan, focus, and determination, I could realize all my dreams and accomplish my goals. After all, the formula was played out repeatedly before me in everything she did. Even if it was something as simple as mapping out a plan to get the most out of the money she had (in the leaner years) to make sure we all had a new pair of gym shoes to start the new season, there was a detailed and written out plan behind it.

Another key component to the winning team was that I was not allowed to say the word "can't," and everyone in the village pushed me (my grandmothers, aunts as well as parents) to do my best. No one accepted excuses, and they had already claimed my winning status. Why? Because my winning team consisted of visionaries.

To know whether or not you're on the winning team, you must know what a winning team looks like. Even though these are things I noticed in my winning team, I believe they are universal to be considered destined to win:

(1) a steadfast 'YES'

(2) the right people in your corner

(3) having a plan while being flexible

(4) commitment

A Steadfast 'YES'

You know you're on the winning team when you have a steadfast 'YES' on the inside of you that drives you to press regardless of the odds. I was taught you have to "know in your knower" that you're in the right place at the right time doing the right thing, and the best way to know is to trust that small voice on the inside of us all that tells us.

When you have that Steadfast 'YES,' you are focused. When you're focused, the distractions that are going to come will not overshadow or drown out your 'YES.' You see things from a different perspective: you see failure as information to get you to the victory and victory as information to get to more victories.

So, the question is: Is this 'YES' one that will stand against the challenges in life, or will it be a distant memory the minute the waves come crashing?

The Right People in Your Corner

You know you're on the winning team, when you can see the leaders on the team. They're the ones making things happen. When you've identified who they are, you mimic their good qualities until you can tailor your own and then repeat.

In my case, my parents were leaders on my winning team:

My mother's path to winning is one of strength and courage. When you look back at the path she took, you can see her footsteps have always been ordered. If I had to name her path, it would be named "Paying Your Dues."

"Paying your dues" is not a bad thing. The generations behind me believe their education and certifications are enough for promotions or elevation. "Paying your dues" is simply getting the experience to be able to see the big picture. The perfect example with my mother is how she worked her way up to being a judge's right hand from the file room. The truth, if she hadn't worked in the file room, she would not have been able to handle the position of working in a courtroom. There were things happening in the courtroom that a manual couldn't answer; you had to have the experience.

In the file room, she handled all the documents related to a case. She knew exactly what needed to be in that file before it got to the file room and knew when something was out of place or missing. Then, she learned noticing, docketing, claims, and closings, etc.

What if she started in the courtroom without knowing what the pleadings look like or the order in which things should be filed? My mother would be jumping through hoops in the background, and the Judge had no idea what was going on. All he knew was the finished product, and she felt it was her responsibility to make things happen. She never wanted him to be unprepared or look as if he was not equipped when he took the bench. After all, there were lives at stake.

When I look at my path, I realize how I picked up on her work ethic and followed in her footsteps with my current position. I learned the job. I didn't just repeat tasks. I would study and learn all the ins and outs of each task given. When it came to working with different analyzers, I knew when something was going wrong from another room. I became skilled at listening to how things sound when they're running smoothly and when things weren't quite right. But, I had to "Pay My Dues" to get to that point.

Even though I was certified alongside several other people at the same time, I was the one willing to run the system in the absence of the regular operator. So, when it was time for promotion, I was considered because of my efforts and success in troubleshooting and making sure the regular operator returned to the office with no issues and no backlog. I put myself in a position of being the go-to person. Sounds like winning to me!

Having a Plan While Being Flexible

You will know you're on the winning team when you have a definite plan (know exactly what you want to manifest) but remember to yield your plans over to God. We must leave room for Him to mess up our plans at a moment's notice. This reminds me of my father and his path to winning.

My father is the ninth child out of twelve, the first of the twelve to graduate from college, and an extremely hard worker. He started with a Bachelor's Degree in Health Sciences and ended up being the lead (and sometimes the only one) in his department for a well-known laboratory. Throughout his career, he ended up earning bonuses and recognition from the company. When he retired, they wanted to hire him as an independent contractor (once he left, they couldn't figure out how he ran the department so efficiently). Over the years, he received bonuses because of the money he saved the company. They were able to take on bigger contracts based on what he could produce.

My father didn't start in the position he retired from. I can remember him working at Faygo when I was a little girl. I have a picture of him in uniform with a cap on his head standing in the plant. He didn't know where that road would lead him, and it may not have started the way he envisioned, but he knew and had faith that one day his hard would pay off.

When I look at my path, I can see the same pattern. I will be retiring from the position I currently hold next year. I didn't start the way I'll finish. I started as a secretary then, a legal secretary preparing briefs for landlord-tenant cases and bankruptcies. Because of my experience with bankruptcy preparation, I was promoted to a position in Bankruptcy Court as a Chapter 13 Case Administrator. I had no idea where I would go from there, but I never thought it was the end. I went from Bankruptcy Court to running a lab for an entire district by myself. It's not something I ever would've thought to do. I really didn't see it coming, but I thank God for His winning plan for my life.

Commitment

Have you ever just looked at your life and wondered, "How did I get here?" Well, that's me right now, and I owe it all to my winning team! Winning doesn't chase us down, we have to get it, and we have to be flexible to move when we need to move. But it also takes commitment on your part.

You know you're on the winning team when you see commitment. Commitment requires focus and tenacity. It has to be frustrating to look back at all the things you started and didn't finish. When I look at my parents, it builds my confidence and increases my faith that all things are possible with God. The best part about it is, when you're on a winning team, you can't help but be destined to win. They've been a part of all of my successes in life by:

- Holding me accountable for the things I start.
- Cheering me on when things don't look like what I pictured.
- Bringing me back in focus when I'm overwhelmed or disappointed.

If the team you're on doesn't have the characteristics of a winning team, start your own winning team. Then, make the decision today to commit to your goals and your dreams. You're worth it!

Remember, there has to be a commitment to finish strong, and you have to finish strong to fit the category of being destined to win.

Dr. K. Olivia Packer is a licensed and ordained minister, author, Certified Life Coach, and Certified Color Code Personality Trainer. Dr. Packer can always be found doing what is truly her passion - teaching others. She enjoys helping others build their dreams and accelerate results while creating richer and more fulfilling lives. She is the owner of the life-changing programs called FLOW10: Mind Detox (focuses on renewing the mind) and FLOW10: Emotional Detox (focuses on being emotionally free). Dr. Packer has been inspired and has the courage to write her story so others will know God's power of deliverance, to be a beacon of light to one who finds themselves in the dark place of abuse, and that no matter what things look like, there is hope in the Lord. Whether it's a short 10-minute talk, a "Lunch-n-Learn" training, a motivating keynote speech, or an afternoon workshop, Dr. Packer's main focus has been and always will be to speak a transformational word into others' lives. Contact Information: (313) 921-6300 www.theflow10.com flownetco@gmail.com

No Longer Embarrassed: It's Time To Let The Secrets Out And Heal

Crystal Sanford-Brown

In the early 60s, children born during that era and coming of age in the 70s, many parents in the Black, Indigenous People of Color Populations (BIPOC) continued the cycle in which they were reared. Based upon secrecy, as a young child, you were informed, "what happens in the family stays in the family."

Parents talking to their children about sex.

Either there were limited conversations about sex or none at all. One might hear the following statement, "if you have a baby before you're married, you'll be carrying that baby on your back like a papoose." With that stated, when perhaps a child during that time frame had zero knowledge of human conception and had only experienced an explanation about a girl crossing over to becoming a young lady, having a menstrual cycle, after reading *Are you there God? It's me Margaret* (Blume, 1970). Many children were out in this sometimes evil, ugly, and sick world, totally unprepared for the violation by relatives, older siblings, religious leaders, school personnel, babysitters, neighbors, other children, etc. Please remember "8" is great, the ideal age to talk about sex with your child. (Steward of Children, pg.9, 2020)

127

Protecting themselves from unhealthy touches

As a result, many children weren't taught a single thing about their bodies or the psychological and physiological developmental changes the child would experience in their bodies. Unfortunately, it's still considered taboo in some populations to prepare your child from infancy by properly naming their body parts; this is your vagina or penis. Those unmentionable conversations can become problematic when children are violated, and they're not equipped to share the accurate body parts that were harmed.

Child sexual abuse is likely the most prevalent health problem children face, with the most serious array of consequences. One in 10 children will experience sexual abuse before their 18th birthday. There is an estimated 42 million adult survivors of sexual abuse living in the United States today. Child sexual abuse takes many forms, and they aren't just physical. At its core, sexual abuse is any sexual act between an adult and a minor or between two minors when one exerts power over the other. It also includes non-contact acts such as exhibitionism, exposure to pornography, and voyeurism (Stewards of Children, 2021, Why Does It Apply to Me?, para.1).

There are two things a child should NEVER be taught, to lie and keep secrets.

Children born between the mid-1960s and early-1980s are considered GenXers, a group that falls between baby boomers and millennials. Gen X is also sometimes referred to as the "latchkey generation," as they were often left unsupervised at home after school until their parents came home from work (Kagen & Boyle, 2021).

Without a child knowing that their body is theirs and no one has a right to abuse and violate their body, adults or sometimes older siblings may take advantage of the child's lack of knowledge and being left alone at home while parents were working. An adult that a child may trust asks the child to suck their nipples or touch their penis while telling the child that they're beautiful. That child may have recurring nightmares, recalling the smell of sweat from the violator's body and unfamiliar moaning sounds coming from the violator while the child feels a sticky glue-like liquid on their body. The ever-lingering fear is present when hearing, "if you tell, no one will believe you. If you tell, everyone will think that you're a bad girl [boy]."

The child can't comprehend the adult sexual acts yet may feel bad about themselves. Loaded with shame that doesn't belong to the child, the child may struggle to ease their young mind, especially during the night hours when the memories of viewing the adult's facial expressions in confusion—not understanding what the child could have done to cause the adult's body to seemingly shake uncontrollably, as the adult continues to touch the child's body inappropriately. The child may want to tell someone to ease these night terrors, then remembers, "if you tell, no one will believe you. If you tell, everyone will think that you're a bad girl [boy]."

There are two things that a child should never be taught, to lie and to keep secrets! When parents do their best in protecting children from harm, that's commendable. Yet when a parent has

129

knowledge of a person's attraction to young children, addiction to pornography of young children, past legal infractions dealing with children, listed on the Central Registry Listing for violating children, that parent needs to have their parental rights assessed for leaving their child (ren) in knowingly dangerous situations.

Researchers used data from the 2012 to 2013 National Epidemiologic Survey on Alcohol and Related Conditions (NESARC) to match people who had attempted suicide with those who had not. A new study found that adults who had experienced Adverse Childhood Experiences (ACEs) were more likely to have attempted suicide in their lifetime than those who had not experienced ACEs. The ACEs included in the study were (1) psychological abuse (2) physical abuse (3) sexual abuse (4) emotional neglect (5) physical neglect (6) witnessing violence against a mother or other adult female (7) substance misuse by a parent or other household member (8) mental illness, suicide attempt, or suicide death of a parent or other household member (9) incarceration of a parent or other household member and (10) parents' separation or divorce (Choi, Dinitto, Marti & Segal, 2017).

How is Human Trafficking connected to ACEs?

Human Trafficking is now the second most profitable criminal activity in the United States (Burr, 2021). In the United States, people, including children, are sold in quantities second only to illegal drugs. They are being sold for labor, and they are sold for sex. Think about the child who has been conditioned to lie, keep secrets, and has been mentally manipulated via gaslighting, that the trauma they've experienced is their fault. Many children don't receive the mental health support services at all. Those that receive the support may hit a breaking point as the traumatic experiences are no longer manageable, creating agitation and a lack of focus on a willingness to live. They may be diagnosed with anxiety, depression, and post-traumatic stress disorder (PTSD).

The incidents experienced by the child may ultimately trigger trauma from their past ACEs, especially if the child has been conditioned to lie and keep secrets. Internally, the child may be too ashamed for not telling someone to request help.

Per Dr. Phil, a child does not have the mental and emotional capacity to navigate the terrain of sexual interaction and can NEVER be held responsible for an adult's violation upon them.

The child that has been violated isn't feeling worthy of their life and attempts suicide, continually engages in unhealthy, mentally, and verbally abusive relationships, and amongst other tragedies, becomes a victim to Human Trafficking. Of the estimated 27 million modern-day slaves worldwide, 50% of victims are children, 80% of women and girls are exploited in commercial sexual abuse. Sex traffickers target children because of their vulnerability and innocence. The individuals who violate these young children demand young victims around the age of 12 years old. Additionally, some parents will sell their children into this horrific and devastating market. (Burr, 2021)

About 93% of children who are victims of sexual abuse know their abusers (Stewards of Children,2021). There are no sacred cows...Friends, relatives, Caregivers, parents, please do a thorough check on an adult's history that children will encounter in their day-to-day and occasional activities. Systemic changes must be made immediately to any application process for working or volunteering with children, where loopholes are present. There should be a minimal check of at least and a Child Abuse and Neglect search, fingerprints, and criminal background checks conducted. For the sake of ALL the children who could possibly be violated because someone didn't thoroughly check an applicant's background, they too should be held accountable.

No longer walking SHAME
As stated by Nelson Mandela in his inauguration speech in 1994

Our deepest fear is not that we are inadequate. Our deepest fear is that we are powerful beyond measure. It is our light, not our darkness that most frightens us. We ask ourselves, Who am I to be brilliant, gorgeous, talented, fabulous? Actually, who are you not to be? You are a child of God. Your playing small does not serve the world.

A child who was molested by relatives is now an adult. She created an inner circle of colleagues and friends that could be trusted to assist with moving forward.

While her enemies were plotting against her, God was increasingly blessing her territory. In 2018, during a presentation to Early Childhood Educators, she asked the audience to select one statement out of six that wasn't true: (1) I rode on the back of an elephant (2) I have PTSD (3) I have six college credentials (4) I'm a survivor of Gynecological Cancer (5) I'm a survivor of

Domestic Abuse (6) I'm a survivor of Child Molestation. A few individuals in the audience responded with what they thought was the untruth statement; most thought the lie was the six college credentials. Hearing the Holy Spirit whisper in her ear, she stated, "they're all true!" Gasps could be heard within the audience.

This would be the first time she openly shared that she was a survivor of Child Molestation. At that moment, she vowed to God that she would graciously accept His assignments to advocate against Child Abuse. No child should ever experience that the monsters in their nightmares are real! Furthermore, God told her not to hold a vengeance against her relatives who had become enemies, that the battle was His. After that presentation, she had about 10 participants greet her and state, "me too!"

Once she emotionally released her long-held secrets to her Mom, her Mom embraced her without shame or judgment. Her Mom shared that she had no idea that her daughter had experienced such trauma. At the time of this writing, her Mom continues to travel with her to multiple requests to present on "Preventing Child Abuse," as her number one supporter.

In June of 2018, the child who once suffered from speech impediments and walked in shame was elected to a four-year term on a national governing board in Washington, DC. On behalf of that organization, she represented them by presenting two seminars at the largest Early Childhood Conference with 17,000 primarily Mandarin Language speakers in Hangzhou, China. With great translators, her seminars were well received by the audiences.

In 2019, the adult who became a victor of Child Molestation founded a nonprofit organization that supports young people who have been impacted by ACEs to see themselves beyond their trauma. She's a certified Facilitator for Darkness to Light, Stewards of Children, and an approved State Trainer so that participants may receive State-approved educational clock hours for their professional development. The nonprofit organization has multiple strategic partners and is a well-received member of their local Chamber of Commerce. She's developed partnerships with large corporations within the community to provide training.

Despite the horrific experiences of COVID-19, the organization sought to provide supportive professional development to individuals addressing "What fuels my passion in the midst of chaos." Again, the courageous conversations have been well received. Additionally, as she continues to make lifestyle changes to offset the weight gain from the multiple medications she's prescribed, she's now a Curvy & Courageous Model.

In conclusion, parents, caregivers, volunteers, please have clear and consistent conversations with children from infancy about healthy touches to their bodies. Please cease using the incorrect names for body parts and use the proper terminology when speaking with children. Have siblings understand that they are one another's buddies, keeping an eye out for one another and avoiding private interactions with one adult and one child.

Your aspirations, desires, dreams, and hopes are waiting for you to step into a field where your seeds have been planted so that you may flourish and pass it forward. I am the child within this testimony. I have become more encouraged, empowered, and enlightened as a result of an ordeal that nearly tore me to pieces. I thank God for taking those pieces and making me whole.

References

Blum, J. (1970). Are you there God? It's me Margaret? New York City, New York: Bradbury Press.

Burr, M. (2021, January). *January is national slavery and human trafficking prevention month.* Retrieved from https://www.mbfpreventioneducation.org/human-trafficking-is-now-the-second-most-profitable-criminal-activity-in-the-united-states/

Choi, N., Dinitto, D., Marti, C. & Segal, S. (2017). *Adverse childhood experiences and suicide attempts among those with mental and substance use disorders. Child. Abuse & Neglect, 69,* pp. 252-262.

Darkness to Light's; Stewards of Children. (2020). Authorized facilitator manual.

Darkness to Light's; Stewards of Children.(2021). *Why does it apply to me?* Retrieved from https://www.d2l.org/child-sexual-abuse/

Kagan, J. & Boyle, M. (2021). *Generation X (Gen X).* Retrieved from https://www.investopedia.com/terms/g/generation-x-genx.asp

McGraw, P. (Producer). (2018, February 28). *A man convicted of molesting his daughter as a child says he just wants her to admit "there was two of us."* [Television broadcast]. Hollywood, CA: CBS

Crystal, a divorced mother of three adult children and three grandchildren, is a retired Higher Education Administrator and Educator and a longtime Advocate who shares "real talk" and addresses sensitive topics in her presentations. Individuals in her training sessions leave with stronger advocate voices for children and their families.

Crystal's educational credentials include:

Higher Education Leadership, EdD(ABD Status); Central Michigan University

Educational Specialists; Central Michigan University, Mount Pleasant, MI, 2018

College Instruction, Post-Master; Central Michigan University

Higher Education Leadership, Post-Master; Oakland University (Michigan)

Public Policy-Public Administration, Master's Degree; Central Michigan University

Community Resources-Community Development, Bachelor's Degree; Central Michigan University

Early Childhood Development, Associate in Applied Science Degree; Oakland Community College (Michigan)

Living My Life Against All Adversity

Leslie Sled

"There is no greater agony than bearing an
untold story inside of you."
-- Maya Angelou

My first thoughts about the subject of this chapter took quite a bit of pondering as to what to write in this anthology. When this opportunity was presented to me, I was more than thrilled to finally connect with like-minded women have some of my compositions professionally published. There are so many aspects of my life that I could share as I reminisce about the past. Over five decades of living life has yielded numerous stories to tell. I thought about all the trials and tribulations, the ups and the downs, the tears as well as the smiles, the births, and the deaths throughout my colorful life. Honestly, it took days to narrow the vast pool of ideas down to a specific time in my life that took place a few years ago. During that time, I was totally unaware of the next string of events that would take place. These unpredictable events would have a devastating effect on the lives of my family as well as myself. Unbeknownst to all of us, my health took a drastic turn for the worst, and my life was literally at stake!

Initially, I was reluctant to expose this particular phase of my life to anyone other than family, closest friends, and some co-workers because the whole ordeal left me feeling very uncertain. I felt weak, vulnerable, and insecure about the future. I felt that talking about my physical situation would somehow disadvantage me to be considered for job promotions or even employable for other positions in my career in property management. This incident could have left me paralyzed, losing my ability to write, read, remember past and present information and other undesirable physical challenges. I didn't want to be judged, criticized, taken advantage of, falsely accused, or looked over because I told somebody outside of my protective circle about some of my physical shortcomings.

I felt a tremendous amount of anxiety while recovering for the first year. That year was quite challenging! I had never been in a near- death situation before. I had never had a major operation in my life. I have never been seriously ill, period. At that time, I was a 52-year-old black woman who was relatively healthy. I was not overweight. I didn't have diabetes. I didn't have high cholesterol. I didn't have high blood pressure. I didn't have any major health issues that I was aware of; however, I did have a high level of stress due partly to being a single full-time working mom constantly on the move multitasking every day nonstop. I've since learned that increased stress levels will trigger high blood pressure, which can, in turn, cause a rupture in the brain.

I've learned how to manage my stress levels by focusing on my health, and I've eliminated some of my daily activities.

I had some serious vanity issues about my health situation. Still wanting to feel attractive and wanted. I'm egotistical but in a good way. I want my circle of family and friends to always think of me as cute, confident, charismatic, energetic, lively Leslie. The life of the party! The talk of the town! The one to show up and show out! I'm known for dance and romance. I flirt and twerk, if you will. You know, I have no shame in my game. Of course, I didn't want that image to change to being disabled or sickly in any way. I was so fortunate not to have been debilitated on one side of my body. My recovery went well. No complications or setbacks whatsoever. I never missed any appointments that I didn't make up. I took all of my medicine diligently. I finished all my physical therapy. God blocked me from having substantial disabilities. Many patients who have gone through what I've gone through are either dead or have extremely limited physical functionality. Unfortunately, some patients never fully recover.

Sometimes when I feel a certain way in my body or feel the slightest unusual twinge in my head, I reflect on that crucial moment. I remember that nice sunny winter day on January 18, 2018. It was Thursday early afternoon when I was at work. I started to feel exhausted. I remember having had some head pain. A coworker took notice said that I didn't' look good that day. Later on, while exiting the lady's bathroom walking toward my desk, I collapsed on the hard tiled floor in front of several coworkers. The paramedics and my family were called immediately. Once the ambulance and my daughter got there, I was rushed to a nearby hospital.

Three days later, I found myself drifting in and out of consciousness, not realizing that the day that I was admitted into the hospital, I had an operation on my brain because I was diagnosed with a ruptured brain aneurysm after I was treated for a mild heart attack shortly upon arrival to the medical facility. I was delirious in a state of confusion in the Neuroscience Intensive Care Unit (NSICU) with quite a few tubes and wires hooked up to my body as the doctors stood over my bed, taking my vitals, and asking me questions to see if there were any speech disabilities. They asked a series of questions to check on my short- and long-term memory. They asked, "What is your name? What year is it? What is the president's name?" along with a few more questions. The only question I got right was my name according to family members. I was told that I kept asking the same questions repeatedly. One of them was, "what happened to me?" Another one was, "Why am I here?." I heard my family on occasion in the background chuckling at some of my loopy responses. I was in the hospital for about three weeks.

After being discharged from the hospital, I had a series of doctors to see as part of my recovery process. I recall having low energy, short-term memory loss, mild depression, and extreme back spasms due to the side effects from the surgery. When I woke up in the morning, I could not stretch my legs out because the back spasms would feel like Charlie horses that would last for about 10 minutes or more! They were extremely painful. Sometimes the pain was so bad in my back and legs that I had to roll myself out of bed, fall to the floor and crawl to the toilet. The physicians did not prescribe any painkillers due to the opioid and fentanyl epidemic at that time. Over-the-counter Tylenol Extra Strength pills was all I could take. The spasms subsided about three months after the surgery. With six months of physical therapy, yearly checkups with a neurologist and a heart doctor and visits to my primary care physician several times a year; so far, So good.

According to medical research, a brain aneurysm is a potentially life-threatening condition that can affect a person at any age. Some people get them from head injuries. It mainly occurs in people aged 40 years or older. A brain aneurysm occurs when a weak spot in the brain's wall bulges and fills with blood. It may also be called an intracranial aneurysm or cerebral aneurysm. When a brain aneurysm ruptures, it will cause bleeding in the brain. It affects women more than men (3.2 ratio). About 30,000.00 people in the United States experience ruptured brain aneurysms each year. Fifty percent of ruptured brain aneurysms are fatal. Roughly 15 percent of people with a ruptured brain aneurysm die before they make it to the hospital! Approximately 6.5 million people in America have an unruptured brain aneurysm. That's about 6 percent of people in the U.S., and it is only when they burst inside your brain that they can be fatal if not treated immediately. Your primary care physician will not check for aneurysms unless there is a family history of aneurysms. An estimated 50-80 percent of all brain aneurysms never rupture in a person's lifetime. An unruptured aneurysm usually causes no symptoms. A ruptured brain aneurysm sometimes causes a sudden severe headache.

In some cases, the ones that survive, about 66% suffer some permanent neurological deficits. Fatalities are about 50/50. After close to a year, my neurologist took me off of basically all medication that he prescribed. To this very day, I am so happy that the aftermath of my illness didn't lead me into the general statistics.

This entire experience has left me feeling very grateful and extremely thankful to be alive. The stars were on my side. I consider myself a survivor! I survived against the odds! My will to live was strong. On the brink of death, I was coming into the hospital alone with being prepped for major brain surgery exhibiting stroke like symptoms. I didn't have any warning signs such as getting a severe headache or sudden pain behind the eye (s). I didn't have high blood pressure. There was no strong family history of brain aneurysms. Unquestionably, I had to take a deep look into my unhealthy habits of drinking, smoking and not exercising regularly!! These are all culprits that would provoke a ruptured brain aneurysm. Frankly, I'm still a work in progress however, improvements have been made. I live by the saying, 'never stop quitting until you quit for good!'

While lying in bed in the hospital room, I thought about all sorts of stuff. I wondered about the remaining course of my life. God wrote my story. It has already been written. It is he who leads my life! I've asked God, "What is the meaning of this incident that has happened to me?" I contemplated the whole ordeal. Everything happens for a reason, I rationed. What message was to come from all of this. What is the real and ultimate meaning of my life!

I am a living witness to God's love, mercy, and grace. God worked a miracle on my body and soul. He healed me and prevented the shadow of death from taking my life! When I look in the mirror to see myself still standing, still breathing, I feel eternally grateful. I am a testament to his will. I am often reminded of that fact in one way or another. It's a blessing to be alive after what I've been through! I love my life and all the lives around me. Taking life for granted is out of the question.

It's due time that I put my best foot forward and live out all my dreams now that I have a second chance! One of my dreams is to write literature. I absolutely love creative writing. I desire to tell my stories, to write my truths. I'm super elated to have doors open for me to reach this goal. I aspire to publish a series of best sellers! It starts right now with this passage.

I've been greatly rewarded with a second chance to live! My Lord didn't call me home despite of the fatal prognosis! My family was told that they might have to make final arrangements before, during, and after my critical surgery. Three years ago, I experienced a rude awakening. I had to take a long look at me and make changes in my lifestyle! Wow, thinking back on that still baffles me. Obviously, it wasn't my time. I'm still here! After the surgery, the neurosurgeon walked into the family waiting room and said to my family, "In my thirty years of being a doctor, I've never seen a patient survive a ruptured brain aneurysm, stroke plus a heart attack; during the same time!." Unbelievable! I'm so glad that God gave me more time with my loved ones. I'm overwhelmed with joy that I have a new lease on life! Wow, I feel like I've been touched by an angel. I am determined to live my life with even more meaning, more purpose, and more fervor! I will be dedicated from now on to making sure that I try to live every day as if it were my last.

Leslie Sled is an aspiring author. In the pursuit of her aspirations as a writer, she writes a candid piece revealing how an unexpected near fatal incident turned into a life altering soul searching situation. Her very first professional publishing is displayed in this book, 'Destined To Win,' chapter title: Living Life Against the Odds. Her story is a testimonial as to how she miraculously survived an abrupt illness and dodged death practically unscathed. She shares her story of facing sheer survival. This is one aspect of her life. Her memoir is in the making.

During her high school years, she earned a full academic scholarship to attend Northwood Institute where she studied advertisement for a year. After switching majors & universities, Leslie graduated from Wayne State University with a Bachelor of Arts degree in Fine, Performing and Communication Arts. She has worked on numerous television productions throughout her career.

As an intern, she worked for Barden Cablevision where she produced and hosted the show, 'People, Power and Politics' on public access television interviewing local politicians, entertainers, business and community leaders.

While employed at Wayne County Commission in Detroit Leslie worked as a community liaison for voter registration, campaigning, poll work, fundraisers, and research for political constituents.

Moreover, she had the opportunity to travel to Sierra Leone, Africa with other business colleagues to implement programs for economic development in that area.

Currently, Leslie is pursuing her passions of writing novels and children's literature, traveling, as well as continuing her path in television production.

A Crystal Clyear Moment
Crystal Wilson

I loved makeup!! It was creative and being a makeup assistant kept me disciplined and very curious about how our faces reacted to it. Different size eyes, lips, brows, nose, skin tones, are amazing to transform. The skin has a way of telling you through makeup how it wants to be treated in a way. There I was, thinking I would be this big-time makeup artist, and I was okay with that. That is when I decided to go to Esthetician school to get more education on makeup. Ended up realizing that I was headed in the wrong direction. Douglas J Aveda ended up being an experience that changed my life forever. Once I started to learn about skin, that's when I realized I made a mistake. Before then I thought to myself, "wow, skin is very interesting!!" At this time, we were working on the actual people, so I really got into it. I was good at doing facials; I even got to do a staff member's facials and that felt great!!!

I believe in multiple streams of income, so I started to learn different techniques and different skincare lines. I studied things that the owners did wrong and right to learn even more. The managers at one point let me run the front desk because they saw my determination to learn all the ins and outs of the business. I did complain of course because you should think about the future. Nothing is ever by mistake, in my opinion. Your why will always be explained to you in the end, I promise!!

When I learned how you make appointments for massages and facials we were always booked. No matter how great the esthetician where it would always be a struggle to get clients. This ended up bothering me because I felt like we were being ignored in the industry. and my goal was to change that. I started to really get into how to become my own boss. My clients would ask me what I recommend, and I would ask God to give me a vision beyond what I saw on the surface. We do more than wash faces! We tell you how to protect your skin and how to treat your issues with great skincare regimens.

At one point I heard a preacher on the radio saying, "do you want your products in big retail stores?" My husband and I went to the service called Global Empowerment. It was a fascinating thing you would be interested in seeing. Some people from all walks of life were there. He was teaching this from his point of view from scriptures in the bible; he was a preacher. I liked it but I still was not fully ready because at first it was intimidating. I decided to go to YouTube again. This time I found a lady named Karen Waksman. She taught the same skills online, but it was too much money at the time! I started to jot notes and kept going over them. I had taken data for about two years. Before I fully realized my calling was to come out with my own brand. I started recommending products that were already out there and decided to see how they react to those clients. I finally just started to research different manufacturing companies that would customize what you wanted in your products. That is when I heard God tell me steps to get what I needed to start my company. I am so blessed to be able to be able to have such an effect on people.

My husband backed me up financially and helped me figure out how much to charge and which type of bottles I should get for each product. I met someone who helped with marketing. This was going faster than I expected. I am still in the trial stages with the products, but people were buying it. I was getting feedback from family and friends, and they would give me their honest opinions. I had to fix my mental health, so I started building my relationship with God. I went to my Pastor and to the First lady, told them my ideas and progress. Ever since then they have been buying my products. I was still stuck at the spas unfortunately. I was not making enough money doing facials and found out I could make more selling my products. One of the spa's allowed me to sell my products at their location. I will never say anything bad about them because that was such a great opportunity. In all honesty I started dreading being at the Spa's because all I would think about was "how can I sell my products?" Then I heard the holy spirit tell me that I could own my own one day. I stayed at both jobs, and I became great at doing facials. I became anxious, depressed, and lost at the same time. I needed to know what my next move would be.

That is when a minister at church pointed me in Tiffany Cartwright's direction!! Guess what, she was the sister of the preacher at Global Empowerment, full circle. I followed her for months watching her journey. I even in boxed her but unfortunately, she did not see it. She put a status up about helping other entrepreneurs and that is when I reached out to her. She said she loved my packaging and looked at my Facebook page and website as well. Mrs. Cartwright got me out of feeling stuck in my situation at the time. I would say that was nothing but God. I was open to changing my bottles and getting the business side right for my business and she did this for me. Mrs. Cartwright taught me how to get my LLC, E and my un codes and Bradstreet numbers, UPC codes, and plenty of other things. I would go support her when she would have launch parties at Walmart. I knew my purpose and that is what kept me going.

I had an opportunity to get on Walmart.com. I tried and made it with a lot of hard work behind it all. That changed my direction into getting into more stores. I started to dream of having a mobile Spa. I met Brandy Ali and she wanted the same thing. I was not ready to leave my job even though it became miserable. I did not think that I was fully ready to take that leap. Everything got shut down out of nowhere during the pandemic. This caused me to go after what I have been planning for. Working on my product line, and making "The Crystal Clyear Beauty Show," an idea that I had years ago come to life; the feeling is so surreal. My stepmom and I started working on a church program and she started learning to edit. I was learning how to be in front of a camera. God was really preparing both Brandy and I what was to come. While promoting my skincare line on all these different platforms I was featured in rolling out magazine. Something I never even thought was possible.

My uncle Eric Gaston was able to help me get the exposure I needed for my business. Working with Brandy got me in the Detroit Free Press. Brandy caught their attention for being the first Black owned Mobile Spa in Michigan! Then she made me her business partner I became head of the Estheticians department... Do you see God was training me to become the woman I was supposed to be? My friends Denise and Shemika have been with me since the beginning, and they laugh at me now because they remember the days I cried and was mentally broken down over leaving those jobs – it feels so amazing now!!! I look at my messages now and see what an impact I have on others just by giving them a facial and great customer service. People say want a facial or they are just calling for my products. This is the process I went through to learn how to make money on my own.

Back to the full circle moment again. A company called SDM saw a podcast I was doing and thought I should interview on one of his shows. While we were talking, I told him about the Crystal Clyear show idea I had, and he said you should have your own show. I ran it by my dad and my stepmother was an expert at video editing and they both loved it and decided to come aboard. She became my Co-host, executive producer, and videographer. My dad's song Crystal Clyear has become my theme song for the show. My brother Condido Jr. wrote song for the promo video as well for the show as well. Man, I love my family and all the support and love they have given!

I took that chance of stepping out on my own due to God was telling me do what comes to me naturally. I did not see in myself what others saw in me at first. To those who have shared or bought products, congratulated me, got a facial, gave encouraging words, those who prayed, for me I want to thank you. Estheticians, use all the skills that we learned in school to help you have more than one stream of income. I will always fight for us because we are just as important as Dermatologists and Massage therapists. We are important so let the world know that you are here. Those that listened to me cry because I helped them see their purpose. Now I try to help others who have that same grind because I see me in them. You must encourage yourself.

I was always told that if you do not believe in yourself, no one else will. You must keep faith, pray, and fast for it. God will bless you! I'm facing the world, Crystal Clyear! 313-820-9405

A Licensed Esthetician who grew up in the city of Detroit, Michigan. She is 38 and married with two young daughters. Crystal went through some obstacles that plague many young in the city. Crystal is also an actress and has worked as a Makeup Artist. As an actress, she performed on stage at the Music Hall and had a small role on the WB "Because We're Men."

Crystal's career began as an assistant Makeup artist and enjoyed it. She ended up moving to the next level in the beauty industry. Her skills were enhanced after enrolling in Douglas J. Aveda Institute and she soon found the love for skincare that is what changed her life.

Crystal loves facials and cosmetics and considers it a gift from God. She has two Pro Seller awards for her Walmart sales and actively sells from her website and vendor events throughout the metropolitan Detroit Area.

Made in the USA
Monee, IL
28 June 2021